Leigh Hunt

A Saunter Through the West End

In One Volume

Leigh Hunt

A Saunter Through the West End

In One Volume

ISBN/EAN: 9783744746946

Printed in Europe, USA, Canada, Australia, Japan

Cover: Foto ©Andreas Hilbeck / pixelio.de

More available books at **www.hansebooks.com**

A SAUNTER

THROUGH THE WEST END.

BY

LEIGH HUNT.

"Quacunque libido est,
Incedo solus."
   HORACE.—*Ser. Lib.* i. 6.

IN ONE VOLUME.

LONDON:
HURST AND BLACKETT, PUBLISHERS,
SUCCESSORS TO HENRY COLBURN,
13, GREAT MARLBOROUGH STREET.
1861.
The right of Translation is reserved.

CONTENTS.

CHAPTER I.

Entrance into London by Hyde-Park corner.—State of the Fine Arts in that direction.—Apsley-house and the Duke of Wellington. — The "Hercules Pillars" and Lord Bathurst.—Pope at school.—Old aspect of Piccadilly, and origin of its name.—Lord Byron.—The Duke of Queensberry. . . . . *Page* 1

CHAPTER II.

Burdett and Coutts.—Cavendish family and Devonshire-house.—Burlington Arcade and French novelties.—Court Yard of Burlington-house, and ludicrous adventure there. —Burlington-house and colonnade.—Why it is concealed by a wall.—The gate worth notice.—Albany; Lord Byron; Monk Lewis; Bulwer; Macaulay; the Earl of Sunderland. —Coventry-street. 20

CHAPTER III.

St James's Church.—Pulling down of the Rectory-house.— Dr Clarke.—Tom D'Urfey.—Benjamin Stillingfleet.—Mrs Delany.—Akenside and his friend Dyson.—Barber Beaumont's pump.—Booksellers.—Fortnum and Mason.—New houses. — Egyptian Hall. — Hamilton-place and Lord

Eldon.—Park-lane and Tyburn.— Dukes of Gloucester and Somerset.—The late Marquis of Londonderry.— Question of rich and poor.— Lord Petre.— Down-street, Half-moon-street, and Hazlitt. — His tea-drinking. — Clarges-street and the Duchess of Albemarle.—Miss Carter. —Jack Boothby.—Bolton-street.—Mrs Norton, Lady Dufferin, and Madame d'Arblay. 35

CHAPTER IV.

Dover-street.— Evelyn.— Arbuthnot.— Mr Moxon.— Albemarle-street and Clarendon-house. — Character of Lord Clarendon.—Royal Institution.—Bond-street.—Sterne.— Boswell. — Allworthy.— Thomson. — Sackville-street. — Duel between Sir Edward Sackville and Lord Bruce.—Mrs Inchbald and Dr Warren.—Her wonderful self-denials and child-like mirth. 56

CHAPTER V.

Regent-street and the Quadrant.—Misapplication of Southern ideas in Northern climates.—Ill repute of the Quadrant and Coventry-street.—Anecdote of a dealer in bullion.— Sir John Suckling, bowls, and billiards.—Great Windmill-street and Dr Hunter.—Windmill on the top of the Haymarket.—Dorset-place, Whitcomb, Princes, and Wardour Streets.—Traits of Charles Lamb and of Hazlitt.—History of Theodore, King of Corsica.—Steeple of the Church of St Anne. 74

CHAPTER VI.

Oxendon Chapel.—Italian taught through the medium of Divine service.—Pius the Ninth.—Rise of the Opera-house. —Addison's banters of Italian songs.—Musical utterance of emotion, a high and fitting thing.—Dancing, bad and good.—Glances of recollection at dancers, singers, and composers. — Aristocracy and Reform. — Haymarket Theatre.—Foote, the Colmans, etc.—Colman's actors.—Planche.—Story of the bottle conjuror.—The famous Mr Maddox, the great strawman.   90

CHAPTER VII.

Addison's Campaign.—Case of the murderer Gardelle.—Broughton's Boxing Academy. — Regent-street South.—Duke-street.—Arlington-street.—The Mulberry-garden.—Dryden and "Madam Reeve." — Lord Arlington and Charles the Second.—Lady Mary Wortley Montagu, and her account of a fire.—Horace Walpole, and mysterious breaking into his house.   110

CHAPTER VIII.

St James's-street and the Clubs.—Wilberforce's first appearance in a subscription-house.—Pitt and Fox.—Hesse and Adair.—Story of Mr Porter; the tying of the shoe.—Butler on gaming. — Colonel Blood. — Gibbon. — Classical memories associated with the district of St James's.—Disappearance of Kelly's Saloon, Angerstein's Gallery, and Carlton House.—Michael Kelly, and his examination before the Commissioners of the Income tax.—Addison's mode of life.—Suicides of Carey and Budgell.   .   .   125

CHAPTER IX.

Abode of Mr Rogers.—Warren Hastings, and other residents in St James's Place.—Cleveland Row and the Duchess of Cleveland.— Sir Richard Steele and his wife.— Horace Walpole at a fire.—Jermyn, Earl of St Albans.—Character of Charles, fourteenth Duke of Norfolk.—End of Lord Castlereagh. — Nell Gwyn. — House built by Athenian Stuart.—Countess of Lovelace.—Sir Charles Grandison.—London Library.—Johnson and Savage.—Sir Robert Walpole and Marlborough House. 146

CHAPTER X.

Pall Mall and the Game from which its name is derived.—Schomberg House and Gainsborough.—Jewish synagogue. The Songs of Zion.—Musical character of the Jews.—Assassination of Thynne.—Persons concerned in this transaction, Köningsmark, Captain Vratz, Lieutenant Stern, and Borosky the Pole.—Bubb Doddington.— His character and history.—Cumberland's amusing account of him. 164

CHAPTER XI.

Sydenham the physician.—Town-houses of the Dukes of Rutland and Buckingham.—Extraordinary adventure in the latter.—Society of Painters in Water-colours.—College of Physicians.—Colnaghi, Strongi'th'arm, Molteno, etc. — Mr Monckton Milnes. — Smollett. — Wedding cakes. — Eothen and Warburton.—Star and Garter.—Duel of Lord Byron and Mr Chaworth. 182

CHAPTER XII.

Clubs and co-operation.—Rise and variety of Clubs.—Exterior of those in Pall Mall and Waterloo Place.—Unoriginal spirit of English architecture.—Beauties of the Reform Club.—Recollection of Laman Blanchard.—Superiority of the spot hereabouts to other London localities.—York Column, and defence of the solitary use of such structures. Neighbours of different rank and stations.—Prince Louis

Bonaparte. — American booksellers. — Record Office. — Statue of George the Third. 197

CHAPTER XIII.

A word on isolated columns.—French Theatre.— Suffolk-street.— Swift and Miss Vanhomrigh. — A word on a remark made by Louis Napoleon. — A digression on American piracy. — Punch and the American booksellers. —Profound and paternal character of Punch.—His opinion respecting the conduct of American booksellers to English authors.—Remarks of the "Times" on the same subject.
214

CHAPTER XIV.

Apology for long digressions.—A few words more in connection with the days of the Prince Regent.—Political recollections. — Success of Liberal Measures. — Indictment against the author.—A costly jest.—A few words more on the doings of American booksellers.—Buckingham-house. —Sheffield and his duchess.—Character of Queen Charlotte. — Her Majesty's favour for Miss Burney (Madame d'Arblay). 232

A SAUNTER
THROUGH
THE WEST END.

CHAPTER I.

PICCADILLY.

ENTRANCE INTO LONDON BY HYDE-PARK CORNER.—STATE OF THE FINE ARTS IN THAT DIRECTION.—APSLEY-HOUSE AND THE DUKE OF WELLINGTON.—THE "HERCULES PILLARS" AND LORD BATHURST.—POPE AT SCHOOL.— OLD ASPECT OF PICCADILLY, AND ORIGIN OF ITS NAME.— LORD BYRON.—THE DUKE OF QUEENSBERRY.

READERS for some years past have shown such a regard for this subject, and been so willing to hear any lover of it who had his mite of information to add, or his opinion to express, that the writer now before them will make no apology to his old acquaintances for entering upon it without further preface. To expatiate, at this time of day, on the advantage of getting as many associations of ideas as we can with the places we inhabit, would be like haranguing an intelligent company on the superiority of a gallery of pictures to a lane made of a couple of dead walls. We shall only observe, therefore, in commencing, that it is proposed in the following work to go with the reader through the streets of the West End, as if the writer and he were actually so doing; that is to say, as if they were lovers of local associations walking along the pavement at their leisure, and noticing any topic of interest which presented itself, new or old.

We begin with Piccadilly, because it is the most agreeable entrance into London, and shall emerge at once from that respectable suburb on the glories of Hyde-park Corner.

The Piccadilly entrance into London is

certainly an agreeable one, especially in the eyes of damsels and little boys from the country; who fancy they see the Duke of Wellington standing with his sword drawn in Apsley House, and the Queen sitting with her crown on, eating barley-sugar, in Buckingham Palace. It presents a scene of house and park agreeably intermixed: Westminster Abbey is a venerable object over the trees in the distance; there is movement without confusion in the spot, as a thoroughfare; and when the town is full, a constant stream of elegant life may be said to be pouring through it and across it, in the abundance of its carriages and horsemen. The quarter also has greatly benefited by the *late* removal of the wall and the Ranger's house on the side next to the Green Park; by the enlargement and elevation of the pavement on that side; the unexpected measure of planting trees and putting benches on the pavement borders; and, lastly, by the retention of the woody inequalities of ground on the site of the Ranger's house. These improvements exhibit increasing respect for natural ornament and for the public accommodation. It is said of some Frenchman under the old *régime*, that happening to visit London when pavement itself was a novelty (as it long continued to be in Paris), he went down on his knees, and thanked God he had come into a country where they had "some regard for foot-passengers."

Yet assuredly Hyde-park Corner is not a worthy entrance to the metropolis, even upon the principle of non-pretension. For it does pretend; and pretends badly. If an Italian were to enter London by this quarter, he would be apt to conclude, with a late witty song, that we really cannot, for the life of us, "make a statue" or "build a public institution." What we do of our own in these matters we do mechanically, or under mistaken impressions;

what we borrow we borrow *in formâ pauperis,* as if in desperate avowal of the incompetence; and having borrowed, we proceed to misapply.

At the Knightsbridge corner of this threshold of London elegance is a hospital adorned with triumphal crowns. In the Hyde-park entrance is a copy of a gladiator-like Roman statue, dubbed an Achilles, which seems manifesting the most furious intentions of self-defence against the hero towards whose abode it is looking, and in honour of whom it was set up. This statue is approached through a screen ornamented with a procession of horsemen, not from Waterloo, but from ancient Greece. On the opposite side of the road is a copied Roman arch, of no necessity whatever, or in the least harmony with the paths about it, erected as if on purpose to walk under (like something got up by little boys playing at arch). It is too big for a garden-gate, and not half big enough as a triumphant symbol. And on the top of this arch is a statue of the injured hero before mentioned, in a bit of cloak which . . . . But enough has been said of the statue to save us from the pain, perhaps the immodesty, of making objections, not anonymous, to a living artist.

And so now, as Gray says after censuring a contemporary, methinks we have very prettily despatched the merits of what may have cost a world of trouble to half a dozen persons twenty times cleverer than ourselves.

We confess we did not think the statue looked so bad, when set up, as we had been prepared to expect; and the arch appeared decidedly the better for it, whatever might be the anomaly of the statue's position. Public monuments of most kinds are full of anomalies. Their only final vindication rests in proportion and effect. "There is no kind of writing objectionable," says Voltaire, " but the tiresome kind." And so it may be said of figures on parapets and in niches, and of horses mounted where nothing could keep its footing but a mountain-goat. If the effect be not displeasing, the means may be allowed. •

The spectacle of the greatest modesty at Hyde-park Corner is the residence of the illustrious soldier whom these objects were intended to glorify. Apsley House is, indeed, a very unpretending abode for a conqueror of East and West. There is no Oriental grandeur about it; nor anything to show his having put down the occupier of palaces in half the capitals in Europe. The Duke of Wellington is thought by some to have been a soldier more fortunate than great; or, at least, of more judgment than genius. His politics were not profound ; and he does not seem to have cared much for anything out of the pale of his profession. The public, indeed, knew nothing of any liking he had except for a concert. His Grace is said to have had a regard for a Dutch painting; but poetry he is accused of having measured by the standard of the mathematician who pronounced it to be "ingenious nonsense;" which is not what Alexander thought of the *Iliad*. His habit of commencing his brief and blunt epistles with his highest military title, made him appear to many persons as one who must put on his marshal's uniform before he can tell a man that he cannot patronise his fish, or say anything for him to Mr Blinkinsop. Perhaps all military talent is over-estimated by the world. A chess-player, whose board is the field of battle, and whose moves are slaughter and conflagration, is likely enough to discompose the criticism of the spectators. But, in truth, few people, even soldiers, are qualified to pronounce judgment on military affairs. The Duke might point triumphantly to events; and till war be done away with by rail-roads, he is likely to receive his full measure of renown. He was evidently a man of great sense and discernment; and if he could not originate the best measures, could be convinced of their necessity; which is none of the least proofs of greatness of nature. As to much imagination or sympathy, it was not to be expected of one who had to execute the roughest business of the world. Poets are not the men for storming-parties, or for the turn of a chance on the field of battle. Probably the Duke did not think very highly either of poets, or painters, or musicians, or of men in general (having seen the worst things they can do); no, nor even so much of himself as the world supposes. He was called "Iron," but we take him to have been of no such metal. The great soldier who could honour the gentle memory of a father who was an amateur of music, and make a point of having some of his compositions played in his favourite concerts, was assuredly (to say it in anything but a disrespectful spirit) a "good fellow;" and we may depend upon it, whatever might be his defects of imagination on other points, that the worn face and lifted eyebrows which have looked out on so many painful and astonishing spectacles in this world, did not behold them for nothing, or were moulded into their venerable expression by trivial or ignoble thoughts.

The site on which Apsley House is built conjures up a curious vicissitude of associations, different from one another, and yet not inconsistent. The first house recorded to have stood on it was a tavern, called the "Hercules Pillars," which seems to have grown into "respectability" from an alehouse. "Hercules Pillars" is a sign (or used to be) which meant, that no habitation was to be found beyond it. Hercules had put up there and planted his columns of bread and cheese, as he did those of Calpe and Abyla. A sign of a like significancy was that of "The World's End." Both are still extant about the suburbs.

Hic tandem stetimus, nobis ubi defuit orbis.
Here then at last we stood, where we had no more world.

Knightsbridge in those times (at least so we are to fancy it) must have been merely the Bridge of the Knight, — a solitary, perhaps undiscernible thing, like the dream of a man standing on the "shores of romance!" Country gentlemen, nevertheless, came through it. The "Hercules Pillars" was their favourite place of resort in that direction. Squire Western took the lovely Sophia there, when he brought her to London. It afterwards became the scene of fashionable dinner-parties, especially among officers of the army, with the Marquis of Granby at their head. The ground would then appear to have been purchased by Lord Chancellor Bathurst, who about seventy years ago built a mansion upon it, which from his title of Baron Apsley was called Apsley House. This is the lawyer who became Chancellor during the lifetime of his father, Pope's Lord Bathurst; and of whom it is recorded that the hearty old lord said one night, after his son had gone to bed,—" Well, now the old gentleman is gone, let us have t'other bottle."

Piccadilly at that time was not the complete and thoroughly respectable street it now is. It had more of a Russian mixture of greatness and meanness. There were three-penny hops next door to a palace, a heap of shops facing the Green Park in which leaden images were sold for gardens, and the road was so badly kept that the foot of the hill was often flooded with water. Among the straggling suburban houses at Hyde-park Corner was a school, in which Pope spent nearly two years of his boyhood. We don't know where it actually stood; but this single recollection will more glorify the spot, in the eyes of many, than all the trophies it contains. It was in this school that Pope, who used to be taken to the theatre, got up a play out of Homer, in which the part of "Ajax" was performed by the gardener.

A hundred years previous to this period there was probably nothing to be seen at the west end of Piccadilly but trees and country road, till you came to old Devonshire House, which stood on the site of the present. Then came another gap till you reached a house called Piccadilla Hall, which was on the site of the present Sackville-street, and was so named either from the sale of *pickadils* or *peccadillas* (peaked ruffs for the neck, worn by the gallants of the time of Elizabeth and James), or more probably from its having been built by a tradesman, whom the sale of them had enriched. Hence came the word Piccadilly.

This was the aspect of Piccadilly in its oldest house condition. A gaming-house and bowling-green subsequently rose on the site of the present Panton-street, which was frequented by Clarendon when he was young, and by other rising spirits of the Court and Commonwealth. The gaps between these buildings gradually became filled up, though with intervals of pasture. Clarendon built a house for himself (of which more hereafter) towards the back of the present Albemarle-street; and Sir John Denham, the poet, was the founder of old Burlington House, which occupied the site of the one now existing. The principal part of the street, however, did not receive its present name till after the downfal of the Stuarts. Up to that period it was called Portugal-street, in honour of poor Catherine of Braganza, the wife of Charles the Second. The name Piccadilly was confined to the houses that stood eastward of Piccadilla Hall; so that it applied rather to the present Coventry and Windmill-streets, or to the gambling and other houses comprising the mass of buildings north and east of that line of road. Evelyn in his affected style calls it "Piqudillo."

Having thus cleared up (as far as conflicting records will allow) the primeval state of this fashionable thoroughfare, we recommence our regular survey of it by returning to Apsley House.

The row of houses adjoining this mansion was built by the Adams, the architects of the Adelphi, whose style may be recognised in the tall and not inelegant fronts.

No. 140 (formerly No. 13 of what was called Piccadilly Terrace) was the last house which Lord Byron inhabited in England. Nobody needs to be told what a great wit and fine poet he was; but everybody does not know that he was by nature a genial and generous man, spoiled by the most untoward circumstances in early life. He vexed his enemies, and sometimes his friends; but his very advantages had been hard upon him, and subjected him to all sorts of temptations. May peace rest upon his infirmities, and his fame brighten as it advances.

In the balcony of No. 138, on fine days in summer, used to sit, some fifty years ago, a thin, withered old figure with one eye, looking on all the females that passed him, and not displeased if they returned him whole winks for his single ones. This was the Most Noble William Douglas, Duke, Marquis, and Earl of Queensberry; Marquis of Dumfries; Earl of March, Drumlanrig, and Sanquhar; Viscount Nith, Torthorold, and Ross; and Lord Douglas, of Ambresbury, Howick, Tibbers, Kilmount, Middleby, Dornock, Niedpath, Lyne, and Mannerhead. He had been Prince of the *Jockeys* of his time, and was a voluptuary and millionaire. "Old Q." was his popular appellation. He died at the age of eighty-six. We have often seen him in his balcony

> Sunning himself in Huncamunca's eyes;

and wondered at the longevity of his dissipation and the prosperity of his worthlessness. Stories were told of his milk baths, his inhaling the breath of dairy-maids, and his getting up interludes of *Paris and the Golden Apple,* the part of *Paris* by himself. The last, it seems, was true. His dying-bed was covered with *billets doux;* that is to say, with love-letters addressed (as Molière has it) to the "sweet eyes of his money-box." He was an astonishing and perplexing instance of the long, cheerful, and triumphant life which a man may lead in this world, covered with honours, and served with every kind of exquisite means and appliance, who has never done a single thing to deserve either, or obtained the respect of one virtuous person. And yet, in truth, this is not the whole state of the case; nor is the wonder so great, or so perilous to the cause of goodness, when you come to look into it. For the Duke of Queensberry, after all, and according to his fashion, was not without qualities which reason approves. He had good sense; was not ill-tempered; not unfriendly; perhaps not intemperate, considering the pains he had taken to secure a healthy constitution. He had always been a great cultivator of out-of-door exercise, an excellent horseman, boater, &c., and he appears to have known the precise amount of the pleasures he could take, and to have had courage and good taste enough to abide by it. This was the secret of his triumph, this the cause of his cheerfulness, his longevity, and of the retention of his light figure. He lived no doubt a votary of pleasure; but he did not die, as poor Brummel did, or the Marquis of Hertford, a victim to incontinence. He showed how much Nature will do for a man, provided he thoroughly obeys even one half of her laws — those which relate to the body. And though he was in this respect but half a human being, and disreputable as a man without sentiment and affections, yet his history may read no unedifying lesson to those who fancy themselves justified in scorning it because they cultivate only the other half, and who endanger the interests of virtue by peevishness and morbidity.*

* The balcony at the Duke of Queensberry's is now done away. The house in his time was a double house, including No. 139.

CHAPTER II.

BURDETT AND COUTTS.—CAVENDISH FAMILY AND DEVONSHIRE HOUSE. — BURLINGTON ARCADE AND FRENCH NOVELTIES. — COURT YARD OF BURLINGTON HOUSE, AND LUDICROUS ADVENTURE THERE. — BURLINGTON HOUSE AND COLONNADE. — WHY IT IS CONCEALED BY A WALL.—THE GATE WORTH NOTICE. — ALBANY ; LORD BYRON ; MONK LEWIS ; BULWER ; MACAULAY ; THE EARL OF SUNDERLAND.—COVENTRY STREET.

WE need not stop to say anything of Sir Francis Burdett, a man whose politics were at the mercy of a perverse self-importance. Neither need we be delayed by Mr Coutts the banker, who could not find a wife to his mind among the aristocracy; nor by good-natured

Duchess Harriet of St Alban's, who brought back the dukedom to the point from which it set out—the stage. Our attention is absorbed by the memories of the great house we are now come to.

Devonshire House has been built three times. The first mansion was pulled down by the first duke, who built another; and this, in the time of the third duke, was burnt down, and succeeded by the present. Lord Pembroke (Shakspeare's Lord Pembroke), Donne, Waller, Denham, and Dryden, read their verses in the two older houses; and the last has seen in it the wits of late generations. It is curious enough that among the various country-houses which the Cavendishes have possessed, their abode in Piccadilly might, in old times, not have been one of the least rusticated, the road in the times of Elizabeth and James having been a pure country road, with hedges on either side, and their town-house, till the civil wars, being in Bishopsgate-street, on the site of the present Devonshire-square. Of no ancient family in the peerage can it be said perhaps, like this, that the reputation for a noble and genial spirit has never failed it. The members of it have almost invariably been remarkable for some public zeal, private magnificence, or other evidence of graceful and generous feeling; and they appear for the most part to have had the suitable personal appearance, observable at this moment.

Devonshire House, towards the close of the last century, was famous as the head-quarters of Whig politics, and for the fascinations of its beautiful Duchess, whose verses on William Tell produced a burst of admiration from Coleridge:—

> Oh lady, nursed in pomp and pleasure,
> Where learnt you that heroic measure?

She learnt it from her race (the Spensers); from their family tutor, Sir William Jones; and from her own cordial nature. She was the nurse of her own children at a time when the practice was not fashionable. The present Duke, her son, though he resides principally among the scenes at Chatsworth, which he has rendered equally delightful to rich and poor, has made the town-house memorable with the existing generation for its balls and concerts. The interior is plainer, we believe, than that of most of his Grace's residences; but it possesses some interesting portraits and other pictures, and a magnificent marble staircase so easy of ascent, that somebody said, "Going up it was like coming down another." The wall of the courtyard is also very plain. But note the elegance of the vases with their garlands. They have a proportion like handsome draperied heads; and perhaps they please the mind by a sort of unconscious feeling of the analogy, without forcing it on the eye.

We have now arrived at the White-horse Cellar, famous for the philanthropic multitude assembled on its pavement, some of whom show such a zeal for helping old ladies on their road to Kensington and Fulham, while others insist on our reading the best daily publications, and regaling ourselves with the finest oranges.

The Burlington Arcade, famous for small shops and tall beadles, is an offset from the grounds of Burlington House. It is a good place to turn into on hot summer days, and wonder how the beadles pass their time. A man may help himself to a complete French education in this thoroughfare. There are sweetmeats to begin with; shoemakers, tailors, and perruquiers to furnish him from head to foot; jewels and flowers to make love with; and, after he has had his hair dressed, he may sit down and read a French classic. Not that we mean to depreciate the advantages afforded us by our gallant neighbours. The late incursions of French wares and ornaments into this country have given an impulse of vivacity to our ideas which they much wanted. They have helped to teach us that colour and cheerfulness are good things for their own sakes; that a little elegance is not to be despised because it is cheap; and that if the elegance is not always in the highest taste, it is at least an advance upon no taste at all. By taste, of course, we mean taste in such matters;—to say nothing of the very finest kinds. We have abundance of genius and greatness among us in the greatest things; but we certainly, as a nation, have not hitherto acquired the art of turning smaller ones to account, and getting the most out of life that we can;—which is also a part of the universality of greatness.

Begging pardon of Burlington Arcade for quitting it with so grave a reflection, we turn into the court-yard of Burlington House, where a very ludicrous recollection encounters us. In this place, some fifty years ago, when Bonaparte was coming to devour us all, but thought better

of his breakfast, the St James's Volunteers, by
permission of the Duke of Portland, its then
possessor, were in the habit of mustering. We
chanced to be one of them. We mustered a
thousand strong; had grenadiers, light in-
fantry, a capital band, and to crown all, a Major
who was an undertaker in Piccadilly, and who
was a very fat man with a jovial, youthful
face; so that our pretensions were altogether of
the biggest, liveliest, and at the same time most
mortal description. A Colonel, however, was
wanting. He was granted us in the person of
William Pitt Amherst, Lord Amherst, afterwards ambassador to China, and nephew of the
conqueror of Montreal. A day was appointed
for his taking possession of us. We mustered
accordingly in the usual place, and in the
highest spirits. The time arrives; the gates
are thrown open; a glimpse is caught of a
gallant figure on a charger; the band strikes
up; the regiment presents arms; enters the

noble Colonel, and, in the act of answering our salutation, is pitched right over his horse's head, in the most beautiful of summersets. Our feelings of course would have been anything but merry, had the result been tragical; but when the noble lord got up, and kindly shook himself, with hilarity in his aspect, to show us that all was well, it assuredly took all the subordination in us to prevent our gratitude from giving way to an uproarious burst of laughter. We know not whether the accident produced in his lordship any peculiar horror of prostrations in the abstract; but when he afterwards went to China, and refused to comply with the ceremony of the *ko-tou*, or knock of the head on the imperial floor, we fear there was not a man who had been in the regiment that did not associate the two things in his mind.

Pennant was wrong in calling the celebrated Earl of Burlington in Pope's time the "founder" of Burlington House. It originated, long before, with Sir John Denham the poet, who was Surveyor of the Royal Buildings at the Restoration. Sir John however had no sooner built the house, than he transferred it to the first Earl of Burlington, grandfather to Pope's Earl, probably in consequence of losses at the gaming-table, to which he was unfortunately addicted. Pennant tells us, that the same imaginary founder rejoiced in his work, because he was sure that "nobody would build beyond him." But he was built beyond already. The speech would much better apply to the real founder, in whose time nothing was to be seen northward, at the back of Burlington House, between that spot and Highgate, unless you caught a glimpse of the rustic village of Pancras.

Pope's Earl of Burlington altered the edifice built by Denham into one of those Palladian villas of which he was so fond;—not always with as much judgment as taste; for Palladio built for a fine climate. His daughter and heiress brought the house to the fourth Duke of Devonshire; and the Duke's second son, Lord George Cavendish, who was afterwards created Earl of Burlington, purchased it of his nephew, the present Duke. His lordship altered, and perhaps rendered more comfortable, almost the whole mansion with the exception of the façade, the design for which by his grandfather he is said to have completed. He retained also the celebrated colonnade in front, which excited the admiration of Horace Walpole. "I had not only," says Walpole, "never seen it, but never heard of it, at least with any attention, when soon after my return from Italy I was invited to a ball at Burlington House. As I passed under the gate by night, it could not strike me. At day-break, looking out of the window to see the sun rise, I was surprised with the vision of the colonnade that fronted me. It seemed one of those edifices in fairy tales, that are raised by genii in a night-time."

> Here Handel strikes the strings; the melting strain
> Transports the soul, and thrills through every vein:
> There oft I enter but with cleaner shoes,
> For Burlington's beloved by every Muse.

It has often been lamented that Burlington House is concealed by a wall. And the same may be said of Devonshire House. The Cavendishes are famous for liberality—for a princely wish to give pleasure; and yet they conceal both their houses in Piccadilly from the eyes of the passenger. It is true, Devonshire House has no colonnade and none of the visible architectural pretensions of the other; but when it is considered what the Duke has done at Chatsworth, and how easy it would be for his magnificent hand to throw up some fountain, or other elegance, in front, and indeed elevate the whole aspect of the place into beauty, people wonder that he does not do it;—not very wisely, perhaps, considering the many uses which a generous man finds for his wealth. If the eyes of the Piccadilly passenger are not enriched, the hearts of the poor people on his estates are. Still it is impossible not to wish that these walls could be taken down.

The loss of one thing in the Burlington wall might be regretted. The gate there is worth looking at. It is the design of Pope's friend, and is no mean evidence of his eye for proportion and suitability.

Who plants like Bathurst, or who builds like Boyle?

cried the poet. Boyle was the family name of the first Earls of Burlington. We had the pleasure one day, while looking at the books in Mr Thorpe's window, which was opposite Burlington House, of seeing in the frontispiece to one of them an old engraving of this gate, containing a caricature likeness of the poet himself, plastering it with his panegyrical brush. It was curious and pleasant, after an interval of a hundred years, to see the print of the gate on one side of the street, and the gate itself remaining to compare notes with it on the other. Through this gate, besides Pope, Handel often went, and Gay. The latter mentions their visits in his poem of *Trivia,* or *Art of Walking the Streets.*

The set of chambers called Albany, next door to Burlington House, was built on the garden-ground belonging to a mansion that bore the successive names of Melbourne, Brandenburg, and York House, from the respective possessors. The first owner was the father of the late Lord Melbourne; the second, we presume, was the Margrave or Margravine of Anspach (Lady Craven); the third, the late Duke of York, whose second title, Albany, gave the name to the new buildings. Here at one time resided Lord Byron; here Monk Lewis, whose genius was not strong enough to survive the enervations of luxurious reading and melodrama;

here Bulwer, whose novels have won him an European reputation; and here once resided Macaulay, who employed the intervals of his official and parliamentary duties in writing a History of England. We mention him simply by his surname, because this is the way posterity will mention him, and because contemporaries cannot help anticipating the style of posterity in speaking of such men. Pennant says, that "in or near" this spot was the house of that "monster of treachery, that profligate Minister, the Earl of Sunderland, who, by his destructive advice, premeditatedly brought ruin on his unsuspecting master James the Second." Pennant was a Whig of the old school. "Sunderland," says Sir Walter Scott, "being a Tory under the reign of Charles, a Papist in that of his successor, and a Whig in that of William, was a favourite minister of all these monarchs. He was a man," concludes the poet, "of eminent abilities." It is a pity, among the many things which Sunderland is thought to have foreseen, that he could not have had a vision of the new historian who was destined to commence his book on these premises, and who has assuredly done his character justice.

Coventry-street, which is included in the Piccadilly line, and, as we have already shown in our first chapter, had formerly more of Piccadilly in it than Piccadilly itself, was so called from the mansion of Charles the First's Lord-Keeper Coventry, which stood by the end of the Haymarket. Its greatest lustre at present consists in its being a place in which, if you look up along it, you are sure to see an omnibus towering over the other coaches.

CHAPTER III.

ST JAMES'S CHURCH.—PULLING DOWN OF THE RECTORY-HOUSE.—DR CLARKE.—TOM D'URFEY.—BENJAMIN STILLINGFLEET. — MRS DELANY.—AKENSIDE AND HIS FRIEND DYSON.—BARBER BEAUMONT'S PUMP.—BOOKSELLERS—FORTNUM AND MASON.—NEW HOUSES.—EGYPTIAN HALL.—HAMILTON PLACE AND LORD ELDON.—PARK LANE AND TYBURN.—DUKES OF GLOUCESTER AND SOMERSET.—THE LATE MARQUIS OF LONDONDERRY.—QUESTION OF RICH AND POOR.—LORD PETRE.—DOWN STREET, HALF-MOON STREET, AND HAZLITT.—HIS TEA-DRINKING.—CLARGES STREET AND THE DUCHESS OF ALBEMARLE.—MISS CARTER.—JACK BOOTHBY.—BOLTON STREET.—MRS NORTON, LADY DUFFERIN, AND MADAME D'ARBLAY.

WE now cross to the southern side of the way in Piccadilly, and return westward till we come to St James's Church, as common-place a looking structure as its builder, Sir Christopher Wren, could have condescended to contrive. It was piteous to see the old Rectory-house pulled down the other day;—to look into the parlours and drawing-rooms that were gaping and smouldering beneath the pickaxe, at whose firesides sat the pious respectabilities of the Seckers and Rundles, the Miss Talbots, Miss Carters, &c. We could not help fancying we saw them there still, spiritually assembled in phantoms of wigs and hoop-petticoats, and refusing to flit till the last fall of the hearth. There also died the famous Dr Clarke, who was more pious than orthodox. St James's Church has for the most part been a very liberal church, as became the good breeding of its locality. Its porch even admitted a tablet to the memory of "honest Tom D'Urfey," which was set up by his friend Sir Richard Steele, to whom Tom left his watch and his diamond-ring in return for a series of agreeable banters of him in the *Tatler* and *Guardian*, which helped to sell his books. But

this memorial came to be thought a little
"strong;" and it was ultimately taken down.
Among the persons buried in the church is good
old Benjamin Stillingfleet, an amiable man of
letters, whose blue worsted stockings are said to
have been the origin of the term "blue-stock-
ing" applied to Mrs Montague and her coterie,
with whom he was an indispensable visitor.
Mrs Delany is another, on whose monument it
is recorded, as her crowning distinction, that
she was favoured with the friendship of George
the Third, Queen Charlotte, and other court
personages of that generation, who were too apt
to be supposed to be the arbiters of what was

Wisest, virtuousest, discreetest, best;

whereas, though most of them were honest
people, they were also very narrow-minded, and
some of them full of mean and bad passions.
Mrs Delany was the widow of Swift's friend,
Dr Delany, and possessed a singular talent for

cutting flowers in coloured paper. She appears to have been a sort of rival, in this respect, of the famous Grinlin Gibbons, the carver of flowers in wood, some of whose performances are to be found in the church where she lies.

But the name among the interments best known is that of Akenside; a poet of rather a formal and pedantic cast, and not so imaginative as the title of his work would imply; but interesting for his elegant learning and a vein of poetic philosophy. Akenside was no pretender, notwithstanding the dignified airs which he gives himself, and which he maintained in society. He felt the enthusiasm which he professed. When he went to Holland in his youth to finish his medical studies, he fell in company with a young English gentleman, whose manners and conversation so impressed him, that he wrote him a romantic letter, containing a proposition little short of the German one in Canning's burlesque; namely, to "swear an eternal friendship." If the stranger had been what is called a man of the world (and he was afterwards accused of being one, though he stuck to the poet through life), he would have looked upon the writer of the letter as a simpleton, perhaps a madman. Instead of this, he made a serious return to the proposal, quite in accordance with the answer of

> Come to my arms, my slight acquaintance;

and he afterwards proved that it was a very serious one indeed, by giving his friend an annuity of three hundred pounds till he could live handsomely on his profession. Whenever the merits of Akenside are recorded, those of his friend Dyson should be recorded with them. Dyson became Clerk in Parliament, and cofferer to George the Third. He was the first to abolish the custom of selling the appointments under the clerkship;—things for which as much as three thousand pounds a piece were given. It is something, in passing by a churchyard, to have the heart warmed with memories like these.

By Saint James's Church is a handsome pump, some years since erected *pro bono publico*, in accordance with the beneficent will of the late Mr Barber Beaumont. It is extraordinary that bequests of this sort are not oftener made, or things of the kind oftener done in people's life-times. But there is a foolish fear in England of doing even the best things out of the pale of custom. Nay, there is a folly which even resents them;—a stupidity made up of wounded self-love and shabby jealousy. In a village not far from town, a public-spirited individual some years ago put up a variety of benches on a common, purely to benefit the inhabitants, and enable people to rest themselves and enjoy the prospect. The " gentlefolks " in the place were angry. They said it was " encouraging idleness in the poor !" We lived on the spot for several months; and, with the exception of children at play, do not recollect having seen a single poor person seated on the benches but once. The poor had not time. It was only the rich themselves, or their servants, that could find it. Such objectors deserve to be sent to the treadmill, in order that they may learn what idleness is.

Between the church and St James's-street are the shops of booksellers of note. Here Mr Ridgway and the late Mr Hatchard for more than one generation placidly waged their political wars, the former with his Whig pamphlets, the latter with his advocacies of Church and State. Here Mr Thorpe poured forth the treasures of his antiquarian literature; and here, next door to him, the "disciple of Aldus," Mr Pickering, delighted his customers and himself with his elegant republications; which, if they sometimes exhibit an enthusiasm for obsolete embellishment a little too indiscriminate, are always pleasant to look at, and for the most part full of good matter.

Here also is the establishment of Messrs Fortnum and Mason, famous for the delicacies of its pottings and preserves, and worthy of the urbanity of its shopmen. Its window is worth notice, not only for the elegance of its display, but for what it suggests, poetical as well as palatable, to the imagination. Here you may see sweets from all parts of the world, figs from Old Spain, and chocolates from New, caviares, and wines, and citrons, and guava jellies, and "jars of honey from Mount Hybla," blue as the Sicilian heavens.

Note the large handsome red houses, that have risen of late years in this quarter, and one of the ground-floors of which contains the shop in question. They remind us of the Flemish houses in the old times of the princely merchants of Antwerp. It is not classical taste, but it is taste very good and appropriate. Good tastes are of many sorts, depending on many circumstances. It is good taste in summer-time to eat an ice; but an honest bowl of hot soup carries the day in winter. Flimsy and pallid houses do not suit the climate of England.

It is a pity as much praise cannot be given to the building called the Egyptian Hall. Egyptian architecture will do nowhere but in Egypt. There, its cold and gloomy ponderosity ("weight" is too petty a word) befits the hot, burning atmosphere and shifting sands. But in such a climate as this, it is nothing but an uncouth anomaly. The absurdity, however, renders it a good advertisement. There is no missing its great lumpish face as you go along. It gives a blow to the mind, like a heavy practical joke.

In No. 1, Hamilton Place, a corner house looking into Piccadilly, resided Lord Eldon:—

a judge said by lawyers to have been as profound in his deliberations, as he was accused by suitors of being slow in bringing them to a conclusion. It is not for us to determine whether the delay was paid for by the depth. Suitors thought not; especially when they died before the decision. Certainly we never beheld a man whose countenance looked more like that of a born judge; one at least made to hold an impartial balance. It was as handsome as proportion could make it; venerable, deep-browed, earnest; nor did there seem an absence of the power to decide; only, on looking long at it—perhaps by the help of his lordship's reputation for delay—the proportion seemed so like a perfect balance itself, that had it not been for his leaning his head on one side, you would have thought it never would have done anything but remain a fixture. To which side the head leant upon questions in general, is well known; and nobody, we believe, will deny that a very one-sided leaning it was. His lordship also, according to friendly historians (for we neither deal in scandal nor trust to enmities), had a considerable inclination to a balance in his favour at his cashier's.

Park-lane is a curious instance of change of fortune, and of the meeting of extremes. Its present name announces nothing but quiet and elegance. Within living memory it was called Tyburn-lane, and was associated with all the horrors which that once formidable word implies. Park-lane was then the road to one of the most reprobate suburbs of the metropolis; and it was often thronged with as reprobate multitudes on their way to the enjoyment of executions, for the celebrated "Tyburn tree," the gallows, stood near the site of the present Cumberland Gate.

A great observer, however,—Pope,—who, as we have seen, spent part of his childhood near the Piccadilly end of this lane (for it was he who wrote the following song in the *Beggar's Opera*), has told us, that this meeting of extremes is not so great as we take it for :—

> Since laws were made for every degree,
> To curb vice in others as well as in me,
> I wonder we haven't better company
>   Upon Tyburn tree.
>
> But gold from law can take out the sting;
> And if rich men like us were to swing,
> 'T would thin the land such numbers to string
>   Upon Tyburn tree.

The late harmless Duke of Gloucester, who lived at the same end of the lane, had a Duke of Gloucester among his ancestors, who deserved half a dozen gallowses. The present Duke of Somerset, who lives at the Oxford-street end, had two ancestors, brothers, one of whom sent the other to the scaffold, where not long afterwards he followed him. The late Marquis of Hertford, of whom a contested will has rendered it no scandal to say that he was as dissolute a rake as Jack Shepherd, possessed the mansion in Park-lane called Dorchester House, from the Earls of that title of the Damer family, the founder of whom was the miser celebrated by Swift :—

> He walk'd the streets, and wore a threadbare cloak;
> He dined and supp'd at charge of other folk;
> And by his looks, had he held out his palms,·
> He might be thought an object fit for alms.

Now "handy, dandy,"—as poor Lear said, —" which is the justice, and which is the thief ? "

The question has been asked by other honest offenders in high places. It has not been confined to the envious or the destitute. A noble Marquis (Londonderry), who resides in this lane, had a brother who, with all his errors (and as a politician we believe them to have been great and cruel), had enough sense and heartiness in him, as a gentleman, to be one of the greatest admirers of the song just quoted.

He has been seen openly enjoying it in the boxes at the theatre; and, if we have not been misinformed, has been known to join a fair Irish patriot in singing it at the pianoforte, with all the honest joviality of a bad voice. We honour him on that and other good-natured sides of his memory; and instead of his dying lamentably of the puzzles and toils of his own time, wish he could have lived in some future age, when poor and rich, it is to be hoped, will alike benefit from a knowledge of the causes that hinder both from being happy.

Poor and rich are alike the creatures of circumstance; but as the rich are in good circumstances, and, for want of the teaching of adversity, naturally enough confound the idea of making them better with the chance of doing them a mischief, they are not as quick as they might be to help improving the circumstances of all; which is the reason why the poor have quite as natural, and far more pardonable a tendency to exaggerate the mistake; for nothing has such a right to cry out as pain. But a new note has been struck in the ears of the world, to which the wisest both among rich and poor are lending their attention; and "St James's and St Giles's" will yet come to know the relationship which all human beings bear to one another. To leave both parties in good humour with Park and Tyburn Lane, we shall take our farewell of it with the mention of an excellent nobleman who once lived there, namely, Robert Edward, ninth Lord Petre, who died in 1801, and of whom it is recorded that he gave assistance to the poor to the amount of five thousand a year. When we go up Park-lane, let us take the taste of the Damers and Jack Shepherds out of our mouths by thinking of *him*.

In Down-street (and in Half-moon-street, which last took its name from a public-house) Hazlitt once lodged. With all his grudgings against the aristocracy, he was fond of this part of the town. He did not dislike the aristocracy when he thought they were on a par with their elegancies, and when they did not confound accidental with moral superiority. No man enjoyed more than he did the look-out of a truly sweet face from a coronet coach. We must add, at the hazard of the anti-climax, that he was here also in the neighbourhood of what he considered the best shop for his favourite luxury, tea; which he used to swear was to be got nowhere so good as at "Robinson's:" to say nothing of its accompaniment, milk-rolls, on which he vented a like enthusiasm in favour of "Simpson's." Hazlitt was as fond of tea as Dr Johnson; and if he did not say as many bon-mots over it, he delivered better criticisms, and has equal right to have his tea recorded.

Clarges-street, which now has so aristocratic a sound, took its name from a family of barbers and blacksmiths, who became ennobled in the person of Elizabeth Clarges, Monk's Duchess of Albemarle; a charming creature, loud, dirty, and violent. She was accused of having been his Grace's washerwoman; and she warranted the accusation by her manners. "You have brought your hogs to a fine market," was one of her flowers of speech. The Duke drinking one day with Troutbeck, a crony of his, and "taking notice as of a wonder," says Pepys, "that Nan Hide should ever come to be Duchess of York"—"Nay," says Troutbeck, "never wonder at that; for if you will give me another bottle of wine, I will tell you as great, if not greater, a miracle." And what was that, but that "our dirty Bess (meaning his duchess) should come to be Duchess of Albemarle."

In this street died, aged eighty-six, Miss Carter, the translator of Epictetus, and once a kind of Minerva in the religious world. She was a very clever woman; but being no genius, is now dead and gone, except as a literary curiosity.

Here too died, by his own hand, during an access of fever, poor Jack Boothby, commonly called "Prince Boothby," an associate of the Foxes and Carlisles in the fashionable world. He was so addicted to worshipful society, that he is accused of quitting the arm of a Squire if he saw a Baronet, and of a Baronet if he saw a Lord. During the last twenty years of his life, he had exhibited the harmless monomania of always wearing a hat of the same obsolete shape. But under this may have lurked the graver tendency.

In Bolton-street resided at one time Mrs Norton.

<small>A Grace for beauty and a Muse for wit.</small>

Are not these names of authoresses pleasant to repeat as one goes along, instead of merely looking up and reading the word "tobacconist" or "tea-dealer," or thinking of one's cares? Mrs Norton, though of an aristocratic sphere, cannot be accused of taking an aristocratic view of the rights of the poor. A fine trumpet has she blown up in their behalf, in eloquent and sounding verses. We allude to her poem called *The Child of the Isles*. Its only danger is that, however sweet and powerful, she has blown it a little too long, and in a tone of too unvaried remonstrance; so that the persons whose conscience it was intended to rouse, might pretend they had a right not to listen. She is a glorious creature, body and mind; and ought to be a princess with a million a year, to enable her purse to flow like her poetry. Her sister Lady Dufferin is another : and we believe that these two ladies are as remarkable for their attachment to one another, as for genius. (N.B. We do not pretend a right to make these or any other personal remarks in our own individual character, but solely as speaking the sentiments of observers in general.)

In Bolton-street latterly resided, for a short period, Madame d'Arblay, authoress of *Evelina*, *Cecilia*, &c. Madame d'Arblay—Miss Burney " as was " (this is the way in which it would have pleased her to designate another)—did not bestir herself in behalf of the poor and oppressed, like the fair poetesses; neither did she partake of their beauty. Sympathy was not the taste of her times, nor did it suggest itself to her comic and somewhat servile genius. In truth, Madame d'Arblay was a worshipper of rank, and by no means either the profound or refined writer her friends took her for. Her delight is to get her heroines into vulgar difficulties. But she had considerable insight into character, and abundance of fun and drollery. The account she has given, in her Memoirs, of her service in the royal household as one of the dressers of Queen Charlotte, whose exactions of attention nearly killed her, and who could not be persuaded that a woman of genius, possessing the felicity of waiting on a queen, could have anything to do with ill-health, is a lamentable, unconscious exposure of mistakes on all sides, and high feeling on none.

CHAPTER IV.

DOVER-STREET.— EVELYN. — ARBUTHNOT. — MR MOXON.— ALBEMARLE-STREET AND CLARENDON HOUSE.—CHARACTER OF LORD CLARENDON. — ROYAL INSTITUTION. — BOND-STREET.—STERNE.—BOSWELL.—ALLWORTHY.—THOMSON. —SACKVILLE-STREET.—DUEL BETWEEN SIR EDWARD SACKVILLE AND LORD BRUCE.—MRS INCHBALD AND DR WARREN.—HER WONDERFUL SELF-DENIALS AND CHILD-LIKE MIRTH.

OF Stratton and Berkeley Streets, which take their name from titles in the Berkeley family, we know nothing, except that they contain the walls which have the honour of enclosing Devonshire House. Yes;—we believe we ought to have assigned the house of Mr Coutts to Stratton-street, No. 1, instead of Piccadilly; for the door is on the street side. But " it will be all the same a hundred years hence." People will be inquiring for the lowly abodes of genius, when the name of the great banker is forgotten.

In Dover-street, Evelyn, the virtuoso, and encourager of the growth of woods and forests, once had a town residence. It must have been when the street itself was growing. His name is pleasant to recollect, because it is associated with ideas of the country, and of gardens, and his friend Cowley. Evelyn was indeed a patriot, albeit a Stuart-royalist; and he was a good man, though a little intolerant and censorious. He was also a terrible pedant in his style; and he did not always subject his curiosity to his principles. He would go to court, for instance, where he must have bowed and smiled, purely that he might indulge his virtue (and his memorandum-book) with a shudder at

Charles's mistresses; and he would accept an invitation to meet such a man as Blood at a dinner-party, in order that he might draw a portrait of him in the same pages with the greater abhorrence. However, he had the merit of securing a proper supply of timber to the navy; and he was Cowley's friend.

Delightful Arbuthnot had a house in Dover-street. He had lived in the neighbourhood of Queen Anne's palaces up to that time, having been her physician; and he died in Cork-street, Burlington Gardens; but we shall generally say most of a man where we first meet with him, reserving a brief memorandum for other places, or such longer recollections as may be specially connected with them. Swift said of Arbuthnot, that he could do "everything but walk;" and it has been stated, that the Doctor suffered his children to make paper kites of a great manuscript folio, full of such wit and humour as surpassed that of all his contemporaries. We take leave to doubt this; being of opinion that what is fittest to make its way into public notice, will do so. Arbuthnot's principal work, his *History of John Bull,* has grown heavy with time. He had not the art of making a temporary subject lasting. But there are passages in it, as well as in what he contributed to *Scriblerus,* that leave no doubt of his genius. The blue-eyed children all born to be reprobates;—the accused people who were spared at the gallows if they confessed they deserved it, but hung up without mercy if they declared themselves innocent;—and the oath which John Bull makes the garrison take, when he captures Ecclesdown Castle, namely, that they were all delighted to see him (thus ridiculing the oaths and faiths of new transfers of allegiance),—are masterly specimens of wit of the first water.

Dover-street is classic ground, old and new. Cowley's good-natured heavy body has probably wended its way up it to Evelyn's house, when the place was half town and half country; and here he may have sat under a tree, on the spot long worthily occupied by the late Mr Moxon, whose threshold is familiar to almost every poet living.

Albemarle-street was so called from property belonging to Monk's son, Christopher, Duke of Albemarle; who, for £25,000, bought of Lord Clarendon's son what had cost the Chancellor £50,000, and sold it again for £35,000. Both these heirs of greatness had got into debt. At the upper end of this street, including the site of Grafton-street, and spreading its grounds over what is now Old Bond-street, stood the famous Clarendon House, which was one of the causes of Hyde's ruin. Everybody knows the story of Hyde, Earl of Clarendon, Lord Chancellor of England, and grandfather of Queen Anne. He was as able and honest a "man of the world" perhaps as ever lived, but still a man of the world.' He was carried by his ambition from the side of freedom to that of power; exasperated vicious as well as good men by vices of a solemn order, of which he was not enough sensible; and was ultimately ruined, both by what was conscientious in him and what was vain and ostentatious. The building of this house precipitated his downfal. Every public misfortune had been attributed to him; the jealous and profligate court joined the popular outcry; and at this inauspicious moment, Hyde must needs build himself a great house, choose for its site the top of the ascent of ground "overlooking St James's," and appropriate to it a parcel of stones which had been intended for the repair of St Paul's Cathedral. Over the windows of the drawing-room was a coat of arms as big as himself; and the inside contained a collection of pictures that were said to have been bribes from suitors. He had scarcely built the house, when he was exiled, never to return.

"I found him," says Evelyn, "in his garden,

at his new-built palace, sitting in his gout wheel-chair, and seeing the gates setting up towards the north and the fields. He looked and spake very disconsolately. Next morning I heard he was gone."

A vigorous lampoon of the day, which probably did Clarendon mischief, contains the following *crescendo* passage, very fit to be sung and roared by one of the mobs at his gate: —

> When Queen Dido landed, she bought as much ground
> As the *Hide* of a lusty fat bull would surround;
> But when the said *Hide* was cut into thongs
> A city and kingdom to *Hide* belongs.
> So here is court, country, and church, far and wide,
> There's nought to be seen but *Hide! Hide! Hide!*

But the pun might be now turned in a different sense; for Hyde was hiding in France, and Clarendon House disappeared. It had not existed quite twenty years. It was begun in 1664, and demolished in 1683.

In Albemarle-street is an establishment which Evelyn would have been delighted to foresee—

that of the Royal Institution; where science discloses secrets to man which Nature seems hardly to have intended his eyes to discover. However, if she gave him eyes which cannot discern monsters in drops of water, and centres upon centres among the stars, she gave him brains to find out glasses for those eyes; so that it is not for man to circumscribe Nature's intentions. Fortunately, he discovers beautiful as well as perplexing things as he proceeds; learns to discover good in the most perplexing; and finds hopes of the grandest and most unexpected sort open out with prospects. The Institution in Albemarle-street, fashionable though it be, and a lounge for the readers of newspapers, is one of the portals of the universe.

In Bond-street, once famous for loungers, and we believe still favoured with a select remnant of them, the more tranquil for a draught-off into Regent-street, died the author of *Tristram Shandy;* that playful and profound humanist, to whom society has yet to learn the extent of its obligations. The faults of Sterne are known to everybody, for reasons best known to themselves; but it is lamentable to see that envy has not yet done with his virtues. Regrets (meaning hopes of its being true) are still heard about Sterne's "canting," and of his want of common generosity to his relations. Don't believe a word of it. Don't believe it, for the sake of the man who has done the world so much good. Don't believe it, for your own sake, who will injure yourself, to say nothing of betraying yourself, in proportion as you doubt good in others. We could relate the most affecting instances of pain given by calumnies of this sort, in quarters whose only fault was an excess of kindness and delicacy. Sterne had reason to exclaim, "Of all cants in this canting world, deliver me from the cant of criticism." Cant is pretension without performance; but people, and sometimes very good people, are too apt to confound performance with manner. They fancy that anything not done in their own way is not done at all. They might as well attempt to confound all languages, faces, and temperaments—a proceeding, upon the strength of which every Englishman might pronounce every Irishman a pretender, and every Irishman every Englishman. And indeed this is sometimes done. People not only cannot do everything in the same way, but if they tried to do it, might be hindered of doing what they could. There is even such a thing as a cant against cant. The best way is to say nothing about it, except in cases not to be disputed, but quietly pursue our own mode of action, and so prove it best, if we are able. To suppose that Sterne was unfeeling, merely because it fell to the lot of his genius to write more enthusiastically about feeling than other men, is at the very least a narrow-minded assumption. At the worst, it is the renouncement of a claim to have one's own words believed. Sir Walter Scott, who had occasion to write a Life of Sterne, and who had no prejudice in his favour beyond what every man of feeling has a right to have in favour of everybody, does not condescend even to notice the charge against him of refusing help to his relations. He contents himself with observing, as simple matter of fact, that his resources, " such as they were, seem to have been always at the command of those whom he loved."

Bond-street has curious memories connected with it, considering its kind of renown. Boswell suits it well enough; but here also lodged Fielding's *Allworthy;* and here, at one time, lived Thomson, writing his country verses. Mrs Piozzi, in her *Journey through Italy*, quoting a passage from him about the sun, exclaims, "So charming Thomson writes, from his lodgings at a milliner's in Bond-street, where he seldom rose early enough to see the sun do more than glisten on the opposite windows of the street."

This might be enough to make some persons charge Thomson with "cant" about the sun. But even had the poet never seen more of the great luminary than in these Bond-street windows, he would have loved and glorified the sun better than they ever did in their lives.

Bond-street was so called from a Baronet of that name, whose title is extinct.

Sackville-street probably derived its name from property belonging to Edward Sackville, fourth Earl of Dorset, who, under his previous title, Sir Edward, is memorable for the sanguinary duel with Lord Bruce, the particulars of which are related in the *Guardian*. The duel was about a woman; and Lord Bruce appears to have been so transported with jealousy, as absolutely to seek the life of his rival. They grovelled on the ground, stabbing one another; and Sackville was forced to kill Bruce in self-defence; for the latter struggled to wound his antagonist even while kept down by him out of pure wish to let him live; nor would that ferocious person consent to accept quarter till he had had the sword repeatedly passed through his body. Sackville was so gentle-hearted by nature, that when his master Charles the First was beheaded, he is said never to have again stirred out of his house for grief, during the two years and a half in which he survived him. One may easily conceive how a woman would prefer a brave man of this description to such a violent one as Bruce. Nevertheless, in this horrible duel, the gentleman survived the ruffian, even in Bruce: for when his surgeon, by some unaccountable impulse, would have run up to kill Sackville, the dying man cried out, to the admiration of his rival, "Rascal, hold thy hand." Verily, human beings are strange, noble, absurd creatures;

and every thing may be hoped for, even from their contradictions.

A certain court "Chamberlain," who is said, in a letter to Lord Strafford, to have frequented the Piccadilly Bowling-green in 1635, has been supposed to be this Earl of Sackville; but we doubt whether he then held the office. He probably frequented it afterwards, while it was in fashion. And Lord Bruce may have been a frequenter of Devonshire House, for he was brother to Christian, second Countess of Devonshire, the entertainer of Donne and Waller.

One person frequented Sackville-street, who was qualified to write as fine an account of this duel as any man could have written; and that was Mrs Inchbald, authoress of the "Simple Story." Her physician, Dr Warren, lived in this street; and she was not only a caller on him by day, but would pace the street at night, purely for the pleasure of seeing the light in his window;—for, gentle reader, she was in love. But she "never told her love." She was, to be sure, a widow, and thirty-eight years of age, but Dr Warren, alas! was a married man; and the love, though thus indulged, was suppressed. If the indulgence be objected to, in spite of the suppression, let it be recollected that Mrs Inchbald was no common female, grave or gay, liable to perils from every deceiver, but a woman remarkable for a life full of self-denial, the rejecter of many suitors, and yet possessed of an enthusiastic tendency to love every good and genial quality that she met with. The following are samples of memorandums in a diary which she kept. She had written a life of herself, for which she could have got a thousand pounds; but she feared to give pain by it. She therefore consulted her spiritual adviser (for she was a Catholic):—

"*Query.* What I should wish done at the point of death?

Dr Pointer. Do it *now.*

Four volumes destroyed."

She supported several relations out of the proceeds of her writings, and would sit without a fire in winter till she cried for cold, purely in order to enable herself to do it, though the savings would have kept her in luxury.

"*Memorandum in February,* 1816.—Many a time this winter, when I cried with the cold, I said to myself, "But, thank God, my sister has not to stir from her room. She has her fire lighted every morning; all her prόvisions bought, and brought to her ready cooked. She would be less able to bear what I bear."

If this memorandum be thought vain, let the four destroyed volumes be the comment upon it. Such vanities are not those of ordinary women, but of women angelical. Mrs Inchbald was not without her faults, as she well knew. She was irritable, and could "scold;" she did not deny even that she had been a bit of a coquette. She did not pretend to be exempt from any frail human tendency. But how hard she struggled and prayed against it! and how, more than was requisite, she succeeded! For our parts, if Mrs Inchbald walked up Sackville-street in order that she might be able to see the lights in Dr Warren's window, it would be a pretension on the part of our humbler self, if we blushed to confess that we have more than once walked up Sackville-street, on purpose that we might be able to tread (so far) in the footsteps of Mrs Inchbald.

We shall have the pleasure of meeting her again. But there is one delicious memorandum which we find it impossible not to forestall:—

" On the twenty-ninth of June (Sunday) dined, drank tea, and supped with Mrs Whitfield. At dark, she and I and her son William walked out; and *I rapped at doors in New-street and King-street, and ran away.*"

This was in the year 88, when she was five and thirty. But such people never grow old. Imagine what the tenants would have thought, could anybody have told them that the runaway knocks were given by one of the most respectable of women, a lady midway between thirty and forty, and authoress of the *Simple Story!*

Divine Elizabeth Inchbald! qualified to be the companion of every moment of human life, grave or gay, from a rap at a street door in a fit of mirth, to the deepest passes of adversity.

CHAPTER V.

REGENT-STREET AND THE QUADRANT.—MISAPPLICATION OF SOUTHERN IDEAS IN NORTHERN CLIMATES.—ILL REPUTE OF THE QUADRANT AND COVENTRY-STREET.—ANECDOTE OF A DEALER IN BULLION.—SIR JOHN SUCKLING, BOWLS, AND BILLIARDS.—GREAT WINDMILL-STREET AND DR HUNTER. —WINDMILL ON THE TOP OF THE HAYMARKET.—DORSET PLACE, WHITCOMB, PRINCES, AND WARDOUR STREETS.— TRAITS OF CHARLES LAMB AND OF HAZLITT.—HISTORY OF THEODORE, KING OF CORSICA.—STEEPLE OF THE CHURCH OF ST ANNE.

PART of Air-street, the whole of which was never much, and the greater part of Swallow-street, which ran into Oxford-road, have been absorbed into Regent-street and the Quadrant. These are great improvements, as far as they concern what has been done away; but we cannot so much admire them in themselves. Regent-street (we are now speaking of its northern portion) is cheerful, and in its general aspect not unhandsome. It has the look, on a minor scale, of a street in Turin. But there is a flimsiness and want of art in the details; and the Quadrant, except in very hot and fine weather, looked dull, narrow, and heavy. The "sweep," so much boasted of, is not sufficiently long or wide to produce the impression which it was intended to make; and as this intention is as manifest as the failure, it has the misery of a trick. Piazzas (as they are called in England with singular impropriety, a piazza being an open *place* or space, and not the covered way that may surround it) are not fit for this country, unless they could be very wide and continuous. The use of them in the south is to screen people from the sun; but here we have not enough sun to render them necessary on that account; and when it rains, a piazza like that formerly in the Quadrant only served to darken the shops, and to make the street look duller and wetter for being narrowed. As to the shelter from the rain, it was for so short a distance as not to be worth mention. It saved nobody coach or umbrella. It did but serve to collect by day the crowd that is objected to in the evening. If all the streets in London could be made spacious, and have piazzas in them as big as the one in Covent Garden, the metropolis would indeed be improved, and rain become a thing to laugh at; but attempts at elegancies like these are but ideas borrowed and misapplied.

There is a sort of poor likeness, however, in this spot to some places in the south; and this may be the reason why it is a resort of foreigners. It is a pity that they appear to be of a very mixed description, for the Quadrant has not a good repute as to gaming-houses, &c. And this reminds us that we ought to have said as much of its neighbour, Coventry-street. In Smith's *Antiquarian Ramble in the Streets of London*, lately edited by Dr Mackay, we meet with the following curious paragraph relative to Coventry-street. After speaking of what took place there in former days, the author says—

"There is a considerable number of gaming-houses in the neighbourhood at the present time, so that the bad character of the place is at least two centuries old, or ever since it was built upon. A curious circumstance relating to this street and the bad character it bears, was stated during a celebrated trial for felony in the year 1839. A Jew dealer in bullion, who bought upwards of £3000 worth of gold-dust which had been stolen under very extraordinary circumstances, was admitted to become approver against his accomplices. The man had two shops—one in the Strand and the other in Coventry-street. On his cross-examination in the Central Criminal Court, he was asked whether the exposure of his conduct had not hurt his business? He replied, that he had been obliged to give up his shop in the Strand, as nobody would deal with him; but in Coventry-street his character had not been injured."

In the same book is a quotation from Aubrey's *Letters* relative to Sir John Suckling, the delightful poet of the time of Charles I.; who, it seems, used to enjoy his favourite sport at the Bowling-green here, which was noticed in our first chapter. Aubrey says he remembers the sisters of Sir John "comeing to the Peccadillo Bowling-green, crying for the feare he should lose all their portions."

A catastrophe like that is unfortunately not improbable in the history of a man addicted to play, which was Suckling's vice; but Aubrey was a great gossip, and therefore willing to believe the worst. The only thing which is known to a certainty respecting Suckling's indulgence in this once-fashionable game, is his pleasant mention of it in his verses. He speaks of himself as one

> "Who priz'd black eyes, or a lucky hit
> At bowls, above all the trophies of wit."

Bowls, as an amusement of the gentry, appear to have given way to billiards during the progress of domestic comfort and the decline of what was called the Country Party, with their field sports and October ales. The change was natural enough in so humid a climate; yet it is impossible not to regret the loss of whatever tended to keep people more in the open air, and associate their amusements with the country. It is melancholy to see the bowling-greens that are still to be met with in the grounds of some old family mansions—fine large pieces of turf, looking like natural billiard-tables on a gigantic scale, and now never used. Billiards is a good game, and as healthy as the house will let it be. It is amusing to hear what philosophical things a player will say of it, in commendation of the "wonderful exercise" it causes him to take, and the "miles" he walks in so many turns about the table. But exercise in the air is better. There is an elegant Latin poem on the *Bowling-green* (Sphœristerium) in Addison, written with all the delicate expression of one of his *Spectators*.

As we noticed Piccadilly and Coventry-street together in a former chapter, in consequence of their forming one line of road, we shall follow the plan in considering the streets that branch out of them. We therefore continue on the same side of the way at present, and shall return as before up the other, after we have done with Wardour and Princes-street.

Great Windmill-street has no greatness

about it, but one large house which was built by the celebrated anatomist Dr William Hunter, brother of the more celebrated John Hunter. The Doctor breathed his last in it, and closed his life with a memorable speech. "If I had strength enough," said he, "to hold a pen, I would write how easy and pleasant a thing it is to die." He had been a temperate and cheerful man.

This street took its name from a *windmill* that once stood on the top of the ascent from the Haymarket. So do cities alter. The miller, in the time of James the First, surveyed the Market of Hay below him, then in the fields; the church of "St Martin's in the Fields," as it is still called, to the left of it; "Hedge-lane," now Dorset-place, running up on his left hand between the two; and the "Road to Reading," now Piccadilly, stretching away between hedges on his right. He shook his head to think that some great men were beginning to build mansions in his neighbourhood, contrary to the wishes of the late good Queen Bess; but comforted himself with reflecting that their households would make their own bread, and that most likely they would not be so sharp-eyed as the regular baker.

Dorset-place, Whitcomb-street, Princes-street, and Wardour-street, are all names for one and the same line of way crossing the bottom of Coventry-street, and joining Oxford-street with Pall-Mall. The "Hedge-lane," of the time of Elizabeth, retained its name along a part of it within our own memory. The now spruce Dorset-place, leading into Pall-Mall, was its squalidest quarter. Whitcomb-street superseded the old name. Princess-street and Wardour-street are famous for book-stalls and curiosity-shops. If anybody wants the richest of books for ninepence, or a piece of old ware full of bearded figures, which he does not know whether he should give twopence for, or two guineas, this is the place to look for it. There are music and print shops on similar principles; and a plaster-cast shop not so proper, for it sells caricature likenesses of poets and musicians in sculpture, which is a desecration both of them and the art. Sculpture should express nothing which the heart or imagination cannot approve. It enforces and detains the idea too palpably on the mind; and in satire becomes malignant. We would as soon dip a flower in soot, and put it on our mantelpiece, as one of these violations of right feeling.

Charles Lamb was fond of this street; and Hazlitt lies on the other side of the wall which encloses the burial-ground of St Anne's. We have heard Lamb expatiate on the pleasure of strolling up "Wardour-street on a summer's day." It was there, in stalls and boxes more precious to him than conservatories, that he found the only flowers he much cared for—

those of literature. His library, which was a very choice one, mainly consisted of old books picked up at book-stalls. He had no predilection for modern editions of his favourite writers, furnished with notes, and costing large sums of money. The notes he could furnish himself, and the four pounds ten shillings he was willing enough to keep; conscious that with the remaining ten, at due intervals of time, he could pick up the disjointed limbs of the great man. His book-shelves accordingly had no outward attractions. They resembled an old fruiterer's, who makes no show. Dust and dry leaves hung about them. But within were melting peaches, and fruit for the gods. The curiosity-shops Lamb did not trouble. He did not care for antiquity, as antiquity; whatever some may have supposed. He thought Diogenes Laertius as dull a fellow as Dr Trusler: and he had as little respect for old bronzes and bonzes, that were old and nothing else.

Music also did not lie much in his way. He was hardly sure that Papal enormities and Italian operas did not go somehow together; though, it should be added, that no man would have been more willing to meet a Pope as a private old gentleman, especially if he liked tobacco. The highest approach which he made to musical enthusiasm was in favour of something he had heard sung by Incledon or Miss Stephens; and during conversations which appeared to him not much to the purpose, he had a trick of humming some Cabalistic verses which he had heard in his childhood, respecting his "man John." But he had an eye for a print or an old picture. Hogarth he revelled in; and he would delight in the high forehead of an old saint in an etching, with its capacity for being " filled with wonder." Therefore in Wardour-street and Princes-street he was happy.

We never heard Hazlitt speak of this quarter; but as he died in Frith-street, he was here buried; and very fitly does his memory also associate itself with the old pictures and books. He was, moreover, very fond of music; and could write things about its inarticulate sweetness and sufficiency, which, as it has been beautifully observed, were themselves like overtures of Beethoven. He would have pronounced, we fear, most of the pictures in Wardour-street to be daubs; and he did not care for a stock of the books as Lamb did. His brain was perpetually seething with authorship of its own. Hazlitt had scarcely a book in his house; or even a print. A few prints would accumulate and be given away; and we never saw either on his walls. Yet no man loved a few of them better. Give him a stroll in the country (for he liked the country better than Lamb did), a room in an inn to repose in, a roast fowl, and a volume of Fielding or Congreve to recall the days of his youth; and those were *his* happy moments.

We don't know what Hazlitt would have said to lying in the same churchyard with Theodore, King of Corsica, who is here buried. Kings he had not much respect for at their best; and Bonaparte he liked too well, merely for contradicting their pretensions and knocking them about. But a man like poor German Baron Theodore, who wanted to be a king, and got crowned with a twopenny diadem, and had no qualifications all the while for being anything but a failure, this was a sort of contradiction of the real and the significant which he could hardly have put up with.

Theodore, King of Corsica, was a poor German gentleman of the name of Niewhoff, who happening to meet with some of the leading persons in the island, at a time when it was wishing to throw off that yoke of the Genoese, undertook to effect the object on condition of being elected their chief. His proposal was agreed to. The German Baron, who does not appear to have possessed a penny of his own, actually got some money and ships together from enemies of the Genoese; was declared king; kept a court for a few months; was given to understand that he must abdicate, or produce more money; said he would go and get it; went, and never returned. He came ultimately to England, where he lay several years for debt in the King's Bench; and he died in that prison, after registering the astonished "kingdom of Corsica for the benefit of his creditors." He had a stone erected to his memory by Horace Walpole. We should not have spoken of him in this summary and irreverent manner, had he appeared to have possessed any qualities for obtaining respect, except the single one of a boldness sufficient to aspire to a petty sovereignty; and this might have been nothing but officious conceit. He does not appear either to have taken his misfortunes to heart, or to have borne them with real dignity. He was a mere strutting adventurer. The worst of it was, that a son of his followed him into England, who, after becoming known and respected under the title of "Colonel Frederick," shot himself on account of pecuniary distress. He was buried in this same churchyard, by the side of his father. A daughter of the Colonel became a distressed writer of novels; and in the obscurity of her fate the history of the family terminates.

The steeple of the church of St Anne, which is a conspicuous object as you go up Princes-street, possesses a preëminence which it must have been difficult to attain. It is the ugliest steeple in London.

CHAPTER VI.

OXENDON CHAPEL.—ITALIAN TAUGHT THROUGH THE MEDIUM OF DIVINE SERVICE.—PIUS THE NINTH.—RISE OF THE OPERA-HOUSE.—ADDISON'S BANTERS OF ITALIAN SONGS.—MUSICAL UTTERANCE OF EMOTION, A HIGH AND FITTING THING.—DANCING, BAD AND GOOD.—GLANCES OF RECOLLECTION AT DANCERS, SINGERS, AND COMPOSERS. — ARISTOCRACY AND REFORM. — HAYMARKET THEATRE. — FOOTE, THE COLMANS, ETC. — COLMAN'S ACTORS.—PLANCHE.—STORY OF THE BOTTLE CONJUROR.—THE FAMOUS MR MADDOX, THE GREAT STRAWMAN.

OXENDON-STREET has a chapel, in connection with which a curious advertisement appeared in the *Spectator* of the year 1711, evidently drawn up by the preacher :—

"This is to give notice to all promoters of

the holy worship, and to all the lovers of the Italian tongue, that on Sunday next, being the 2d of December, at five in the afternoon, in Oxendon Chapel, in Oxendon-street, near the Haymarket, there will be divine service in the Italian tongue, and will continue every Sunday at the aforesaid hour, with an Italian sermon preached by Mr Cassotti, Italian minister, author of a new method of teaching the Italian tongue to ladies," &c.

How far "the holy worship" and the Italian tongue served to promote one another, we are not told. The ladies, we fear, would have been so much more absorbed in genitive and dative cases than in those of conscience, that their mothers would hardly let them go. There is one Italian preacher now living, and one only, whose matter we can suppose to predominate over his manner, sweet as that may be; and that is, the Pope;—a glorious being, if he can but continue as he has begun;—glorious indeed, if only for having begun.

We have already seen how the appellation of "Haymarket" originated, and how it has ceased to be applicable. But the meaning of a name is seldom thought of by the person that utters it. Who thinks of chickens when he is entering the "Poultry?" or of a place by the water-side, when he mentions "the Strand?" All the ideas associated with the Haymarket are those of the "Little Theatre" and the "Opera House;" and delightful ideas they are.

To begin, as in politeness and chronology bound, with the foreigner. A school for the Italian language was here set up to some purpose. The Queen's Theatre originated with Vanbrugh, its first architect. The foundation-stone, agreeably to the gallantry of those times, was inscribed with the words "Little Whig," in honour of the reigning toast, Anne,

Countess of Sunderland, one of the daughters of Marlborough. Vanbrugh began the performances with a translated Italian Opera, which did not succeed. He followed this with his own comedies, which, excellent as they were, succeeded as little, owing to the size of the house, which rendered them inaudible. Italian operas then took exclusive possession of the place, ultimately accompanied by the ballet as we now see it; and it was probably to the jealousy occasioned among Vanbrugh's friends by the prosperity of Italian singing, that we owe the amusing but mistaken banters of it in the *Spectator* from the pen of Addison, who was a great wit, but had no taste for music. It is impossible to help laughing at the melodious tyrants and dulcet murderers which he delighted to describe; still more so at the mock-Italian song in the *Guardian*:—

"Oh, what joys our prospects yield!
Charming joys our prospects yield!

>In a new *livery*
>When we see *every*
>Bush and meadow, tree and field.
>Then how sweet it is to dream!
>*Charming* sweet it is to dream
>On mossy pillows
>By the *tirilloes*
>Of a gently murmuring stream," &c.

But Addison (with leave be it said), not knowing anything of music, nor indeed of Italy except as classical ground, though he had travelled in it, saw neither the natural connection which exists between common speech and recitative in the beautiful Italian language, nor the warrantableness, nay, the propriety, in a high ideal sense, with which the eloquence of passion is shaped into the beauty natural to all truth and energy by the beauty of music. The Italian Opera prospered, not, as Addison thought, in spite of truth, but in exaltation of it. The ridicule would have been better directed at the ballet, or rather at the French and more mechanical portion of it, its posture-making, twirling, and presentation of legs to the sideboxes; for a truth of a different and very unideal sort was the secret of the success of that. Yet there is a beautiful ideal in the ballet also, including even the better sort of the French portion of it (which may be called the Watteau, or artificial-natural portion), and ascending through the passion of the Spanish dance up to the highest heaven of Italian grace and composure. Common French opera-dancing, with its stiff dapper set-out of muslin and gauze, its spinning and twirling, its making of cheeses (as the little girls call the subsiding of their whirled petticoats), or rather its half Dutch-cheeses ready made, its ultra smiling or serious faces, and its extraordinary mathematical studies of right angles, with one foot at rest and the other in the air, looks like a milliner run mad for conceit, and unable to express the sense of her perfections. When superior to this, the French Terpsichore is a damsel still artificial, and a little unaccountable; but very agreeable withal, often elegant, sometimes even graceful. Spanish dancing is the intoxication of pleasure and animal spirits. Perhaps it is the only perfect dancing in the world, if we are to look upon dancing as a thing thoroughly accountable to nature as well as art. But the highest mixture of French and Italian dancing, or the combination of mechanical mastery and ideal grace, at once voluptuous and decent, is what is looked upon as the crown of the art, and intoxicates adoring multitudes with the Elslers and Taglionis.

It is difficult to walk by the Opera House, and not have the memory crowded with these ladies and their partners;—with the Taglionis, and Ceritos, and Heberles;—the Vestrises, Angiolinis, Dehayes, Labories, Presles, and Parisots. A whole tinsel heaven of artificial flowers, French abbés, and powdered beaux opens out in the distance. The Duke of Queensberry is distracted where to fix his "heart;" and now and then a heart is really touched by some honest girl, whose mother is anxiously waiting to take her home, and whose beauty is, his Grace thinks, insipid.

But though dancing is perhaps more than half the secret of the attraction of the Opera House, and fashion constitutes no small part of the remainder, music is its great honour and glory; divine singing and diviner composition. Here Farinelli has sung, whom the ladies deified in profane speeches; here Nicolini, who charmed even Addison; here Senesino, who made a man that was acting a tyrant forget his part, and embrace him on the stage; here, in our own days, handsome Trammezzani, and humorous Naldi, and *Don Juan* Ambrogetti, who for all his stout calves went into La Trappe (so much earnestness is at the heart of these supposed triflers), and warbling Rubini, and all-accomplished Lablache, with a voice worthy of the Phidian Jupiter, and delightful Malibran, and voluptuous Grassini, and Pasta the divine, who was all truth to nature and passion, if not always to *B in alt*. Here also Handel has been in person, wielding his thunderbolts; and Sacchini with his dulcet airs; and Mozart when a child, perhaps thinking how he should rule there by and by; and Winter with his lovely *Ratto di Proserpina* (for her performance in which he was seen to stoop his tall person in the green room, and kiss the hand of Mrs Billington); and Rossini, who runs almost the whole round of his art, from the giddiest animal spirits up to the grandeurs of devotion.

When an Opera night is at its very best, with fine singing, fine acting, fine dancing, and a crowd of visitors including the most tasteful part of the aristocracy with their handsome and serene countenances, it is so far from being the false and vicious thing which bigots pretend, that on the contrary (not to say it irreverently, and allowing for the due mixture of frailty in all human assemblages), it is a triumphant specimen of what Nature herself can do in the way of art and prosperity, and what all the world may hope to partake, in proportion as knowledge and elegance are diffused. The "young ladies" of humbler life (as all school-taught and pianoforte-playing females are now called, and not improperly, whatever Cobbett chose to fulminate to the contrary), are a far superior race to the loud and coarse-minded generation that preceded them; and as society advances, what is to hinder refinement from being farther extended, or refinement itself from being purified of the spots in its character occasioned by its confounding itself with exclusiveness and privilege? At all events, advance society must; and in what better spirit can it advance, than in that of recognizing all true things for what they are, the ornamental as well as the useful, and doing its best to confirm and partake them? That prosperity (supposing it to do so) should exist only in corners, is lamentable. But what then? Are we to quarrel with the corners? No, we are to extend the prosperity. This is what all the wise and witty reformers of the day emphatically think, we may rest assured, whatever their gibes may occasionally appear to say to the contrary. All Anti-*Snobbism* in particular (that admirable discovery) is a weeder, not a destroyer; and it weeds everywhere, not in one place only. True reformers level as advancement does; not by pulling down, but by raising up.

The Opera House has been often rebuilt, and is now a pleasing though not remarkable structure.

But we must hasten away from this tempting subject, and cross to the native Theatre on the opposite side of the street. The "Theatre Royal, Haymarket," or, as it used to be called, the "Little Theatre," to distinguish it from its big neighbour, arose not long after the appearance of the other, on the site of the "King's Head Inn," probably the resort of the Haydealers. It professed to be intended for "French players," and opened accordingly with a French comedy. It appears however to have been used for any kind of entertainment that would attract visitors, including rope-dancing and tumbling. Foote then hired it for what he called his Tea-parties, which were monologues of witty lampoon, disguised under that title in order to evade the statute; for he had no license. Obtaining a license in the year 1767, this diverting but unprincipled writer pulled down and rebuilt the theatre, for the performance of his comedies; and this was the edifice that stood till the year 1820, when the present one was erected from a design of Mr Nash. It is one of the best of all his buildings, for it aimed at nothing original. The portico is Corinthian; and the whole being in good proportion, both with itself and the neighbouring objects, forms a real ornament to the street.

Perhaps there never was any theatre in England associated with such an incessant stream of lively recollections as this. Foote began it with his laughable satires; the two Colmans, father and son, followed with comedy and farce, including those of Mrs Inchbald and O'Keefe; then came Thomas Dibdin and Morris, both good caterers; and Webster, with his pieces and afterpieces from the French, and his coadjutor Planché, who prospers in everything he does, has turned half the fairy tales into the most amusing verse.

The Haymarket Theatre is a summer theatre, though it contrives to crib a good bit out of the other seasons. We recollect well the old house in the time of Colman, junior; and a most inconvenient, unbearable, " stived up," hot, laughing, delicious place it was. You went there with your thoughts full of the *Heir-at-Law*, or the *Wags of Windsor;* of Elliston, Munden, or Fawcett; complained of the heat the first ten minutes, and forgot it afterwards in one melting bath of song, joke, and laughter. Who that enjoyed could ever forget the knife-grinding merriment of the tones of Fawcett; the intense grimaces of Munden, making something out of nothing; the genial fervour of Elliston, the only man who knew how to make love; the lack-a-daisical vigour and good singing of "Irish Johnstone;" Emery's Yorkshiremen; delightful little ballad-singing Bland, fat and swarthy, with a tone of trusting sweetness; and Mrs Gibbs in her pastoral days, with her pretty fair face and black mittens? Other names are as famous, but we associate them more with other theatres. These were the heroes and heroines of those pieces by Colman which almost exclusively occupied the stage during his management, and which vindicated the exclusiveness by their popularity. We have not been so well acquainted with the theatre of late years; but when chance has taken us there, we have expected something pleasant as a matter of course, and do not remember to have been disappointed.

It was at this theatre, during its first period, that the famous imposition took place, called the Bottle Conjuror. It was said to have been a contrivance of the Duke of Montagu (John Montagu, second Duke), who was too much addicted to hoaxes. Advertisements appeared, announcing that a man on such an evening would get into a quart bottle on the stage, and sing a song in it. A house assembled, so crowded that multitudes could not get in. The audience waited to no purpose. At last somebody came forward and said the money should be returned if the gentleman did not come; to which some facetious fellow added, that the gentleman would get into a *pint* bottle for double prices. Their impatience now rose into fury; they smashed the candlesticks, tore up the benches, and so went home like simpletons as they were, thinking they had done a fine thing by adding folly to folly.

It is the custom in relating this story to speak of the credulity as a thing " incredible." But some persons may have gone out of a reasonable curiosity to know how such an imposition would be taken. Others might think it some wonderful piece of art, after the fashion of the jugglers in India. And as to the many, what right have we to be astonished at any amount of credulity in human beings? The feeling is natural enough undoubtedly, unavoidable; but a little consideration checks it. Those who express the astonishment most, cherish in all probability some credulities of their own, quite as empty as the conjuror's bottle; and it is only by a knowledge of our like common tendency that we acquire a right to be astonished at all. In truth, credulity is but the wrong side of a very right thing—a sense of the limits of our knowledge. The main point with all of us is to take care that we do not pervert a thing so modest, either into an arrogant determination of those limits, or into a foolish encouragement of assumption, in people who are no more conjurors than ourselves.

But we fear we have been indulging in that dreadful and most unnecessary of all *bores*, the " moral " after the story.

We must not quit the Haymarket Theatre without noticing the " famous Mr Maddox," the most wonderful achiever of balances, " under difficulties," who made a fortune here about eighty years ago. He danced on wire, and did all sorts of impossible things with straws, eggs, wine-glasses, and tobacco-pipes. The following are samples from his advertisements :—

"Stands with one foot on the wire, balances a straw on the edge of a glass, and plays on the fiddle at the same time."

"Will set a table across the wire, and perform a table-dance with three pewter plates."

"Stands on his head on the wire in full swing."

"Tosses and catches a straw on different parts of his face, and from his left to his right shoulder, from thence to his knees down to his feet, tosses it up again to his forehead, and from thence to his right heel, then holds a wine-glass in his mouth, and tosses the straw with his heel into the glass; takes the straw with the ear downwards, and with a blast blows it topsy-turvy."

This illustrious performer on the straw appears to have been the "star" of the greatest magnitude that ever drew crowds to a theatre.

He fairly "dwells apart" in the annals of stage profits. He made (and he made it, observe, in days when the sum was far greater than now) £11,000 in one season; "which," says our informant, Mr Smith, "is £2500 more than Garrick's, a few years previous." This is the greatest blow to the vanity of public fortune-making that we ever read of. Goldsmith, who condescended to be jealous of all stage performers, from "Polly and the pickpocket" (as he called those in the *Beggar's Opera*) down to the heroes of a puppet-show (not considering that his fine genius was made cheap by printing, and was of a nature to be immortal), might fairly have died of Mr Maddox. A straw chucked from shoulder to shoulder at the rate of twenty guineas a time! Head of Fo! What would Confucius have thought of it! It is to be allowed that Mr Maddox's perseverance must have been great, and that the ingenuity of his shoulder-blades deserved attention, whatever might have been said to their opulence. The probability is, however, that with such tangible proofs of attractiveness in his account-books, Mr Maddox took himself for a great man, and drove about in his carriage with an air of dignity.

CHAPTER VII.

ADDISON'S CAMPAIGN.—CASE OF THE MURDERER GARDELLE.—BROUGHTON'S BOXING ACADEMY. — REGENT STREET SOUTH. — DUKE STREET. — ARLINGTON STREET. — THE MULBERRY GARDEN.—DRYDEN AND "MADAM REEVE."—LORD ARLINGTON AND CHARLES THE SECOND.—LADY MARY WORTLEY MONTAGU, AND HER ACCOUNT OF A FIRE.—HORACE WALPOLE, AND MYSTERIOUS BREAKING INTO HIS HOUSE.

POPE, walking one day in the Haymarket, with Harte, took him through a little shop up three pair of stairs into a garret, and said, "In this garret Addison wrote his Campaign." Addison was then young, and at the lowest ebb of his fortunes; but he had a link with the Government. He was encouraged to celebrate Marlborough's victory at Blenheim, and the minister took the author out of his garret, and made him Commissioner of Appeals. We shall not stop to inquire whether Addison or Mr Maddox was the better paid in this instance. The Campaign is certainly not a poem that could have cost the writer much wear and tear of feeling; but the ministers beheld in him a man of genius, who had served their cause; and posterity is grateful to them for making the mind easy which subsequently produced the delightful *Spectator*.

By way of giving people the full benefit of a hardening spectacle, murderers used to be hung all over London; that is to say, on the spots where they committed the deed; or, if the place was not open and satisfactory enough, on the nearest spot most convenient. This was the case with a Frenchman of the name of

Gardelle, an artist in enamel, who, having murdered a female, disposed of her body in the manner that not long since horrified the public in the case of Greenacre. Gardelle lived in one of the streets leading to Leicester Square, and was executed in the Haymarket. He appears to have been a clever man, and probably had obtained a respect which he could not bear to part with. "To seem and not to be"—the principle of too many respectable people—is carried to a pitch of insanity by these deplorable wretches. They appear to be wanting in some moral perception, common to the rest of the community; just as others want the sense of smelling or tasting. There is an instinctive wisdom in popular phrases; and one of these seems to designate such men justly when it describes them as "ill-contrived." Indeed, they generally, perhaps always, exhibit some malformation of skull; as may be seen by the phrenological casts in the shop windows. They are not to be looked upon as thoroughly human beings.

Gardelle's execution probably took place at the northern end of the Haymarket. At the southern end, between the Little Theatre and Cockspur-street, was the Boxing Academy of the famous Broughton, the prize-fighter. In one of his bills, "Frenchmen" were requested "to bring smelling bottles." So strangely constituted are the "ill-contrived," and so effeminate, often, the brutal, that perhaps Gardelle himself would have needed such a bottle, had he gone to see the fighting. This anti-Gallican insult, however, was inspired by the long series of Marlborough victories. They encouraged the same ill manners in us up to the period of the revolutionary wars; when, after taunting the French for half a century with their "wooden shoes," and their servility to the "Grand Monarque," and then trying our utmost to keep them confined to both, we discovered, that to calumniate a great nation any longer was neither worthy of us, nor very easy.

Adieu to strange, pleasant, theatrical, opera-singing, execution-insulted Haymarket, with no meaning any longer in its name, but as sweet, taking it all in all, as the fragrance that was once in its thoroughfare. We are desirous of getting through Piccadilly, and coming to still more attractive quarters: but the west end of the metropolis is thronged with memories, and we find ourselves arrested at every step by some agreeable or some melancholy face.

The southern portion of Regent-street is wider and handsomer than the northern: had it all been built on the same scale, something might have been said of it; but the hearts of Englishmen, which are so bold when rough work is to be done and blood expended, are apt to quail at the thought of any gentler magnificence. They are desirous to beat all other nations in every species of greatness; but when the conquest is to be achieved on the side of the fine arts, they break down in the attempt, and look foolish, like people conscious of having no call that way:—dancers, who have never learnt to dance:—lovers, who take a lady into a shop for the purpose of presenting her with some jewellery, and finish by requesting her acceptance of a dozen albata spoons.

Regent-street South, nevertheless, is full of the abodes of architects; and, in the general interior of its houses, it is a comprehensive specimen of the activity and prosperity of the most flourishing portion of society, not excluding its advancement. It has bishops in it, and noblemen; abounds in lawyers, dress-makers, army and other clothiers, in chambers and clubs; and it comprises philosophical and statistical societies, and companies of steam navigation. A physical or moral voluptuary might enjoy the whole round of English luxury and information within the compass of this street (supported by the patent stomach-pump on one side of the way, and the fire-insurance office on the other), and book himself next morning for Greece or the Pyramids.

In Duke-street, about forty years ago, died an artist, who was about to originate an exhibition of a kind which it is a pity has never taken place, and which, supposing it to be well executed, we cannot but think would be interesting; namely, a gallery of copies from great masters. We are surprised too, or rather, we lament, that such copies are not more in request by the rich. We have seen admirable ones, which any man of taste would be happy to possess, and which far surpassed, of course, the finest engravings; engravings being of necessity small and colourless. The artist we allude to was named Head, the same, we presume, who is to be met with as "Guido Head," the designer of a well-known print of "Echo." His death was attended, perhaps caused, by some circumstances of a singularly distressing nature. He went out to call upon an intimate friend, who had died a few hours before his arrival. Returning home much affected, he found that one of his daughters, whom he had left in apparent health, had died during his absence. He took to his bed, and followed her in three days.

We speak of Arlington-street before St James's-street, because the latter will take us away from the Piccadilly quarter into St James's Park and the palaces. Arlington-street is so called from Henry Bennett, Earl of Arlington, one of the unprincipled Cabal Administration in the time of Charles the Second. It occupies part of the site of the once famous Mulberry Gardens, a place of entertainment which gave a title to one of Sedley's plays, and which included a portion of St James's Park and of the present Green Park. Dryden had been seen there with "Madame Reeve," the actress, eating tarts; "no inelegant pleasure," quoth Sir Walter Scott. Bennett obtained the expired lease of the Gardens, and turned them into a house and grounds of his own, the beauties of which were celebrated in Latin verse by Charles Dryden, son of the poet. The Mulberry Gardens was a place to which people of fashion resorted, and ladies came in masks, to sit in arbours and eat syllabubs; and this scene, on a small scale, was probably continued in the grounds of Henry Bennett, whose whole object, as his motto intimated, was to do His Majesty service (*De bon vouloir servir le Roi*). The King was a frequent guest of his Lordship's. The Gardens had a wilderness, which the noble lord retained, probably the spot lately so called near the rails in Piccadilly; and his poet expressly informs us, in his most ingenuous manner, that this wilderness was still frequented by lovers.*

Arlington-street has been one of the head-quarters of fashion ever since it existed. It is half filled now, as it has always been, with mansions of the nobility. These look on the Green Park; and their gardens, in all probability, however altered, are remnants of the scenes of Dryden's and King Charles's courtships. A "mount," which the poet's son alludes to as standing at the end of Bennett's garden, and constituting a favourite resort of the long and swift legs of his royal visitor, was perhaps no loftier spot than the ascent partly remaining by the Piccadilly rails. It would enable the "merry king," who, with all his faults, was no scorner of those beneath him, to give a look over the wall and see what was going forward among the public-houses of his beloved sub-

* " Securi hic tenero ludunt in gramine amantes."

jects, on the spot since illustrated by the corresponding visage of the Duke of Queensberry.

Charles was at the height of his passion for the Duchess of Portsmouth at the time when Bennett obtained the lease of these crown lands. The noble lord was one of the political go-betweens who brought about the connexion with the beautiful Frenchwoman, then Mademoiselle de Querouaille. Charles created her a Duchess the year following; and so curiously do events hold together in this world, that, on the spot where the king and his mistress then visited, afterwards lived his descendant from her son the Duke of Richmond, Charles Fox.

Lady Mary Wortley Montagu resided in Arlington-street before she was married. Her father, the Duke of Kingston (then Marquis of Dorchester), had a house there. Her Ladyship, in one of her virgin letters to her friend Mrs Hewet, gives the following lively account of a fire which took place in the street:—

"The fire, I suppose, you have had a long and true account of, though not perhaps that we were raised at three o'clock and kept waiting till five by the most dreadful sight I ever saw in my life. It was near enough to fright all our servants out of their senses; however we escaped better than some of our neighbours. Mrs Braithwayte, a Yorkshire beauty, who had been but two days married to a Mr Coleman, ran out of bed *en chemise*, and her husband followed her in his, in which pleasant dress they ran as far as St James's-street, where they met with a chair and prudently crammed themselves both into it, observing the rule of dividing the good and bad fortune of this life, resolved to run all hazards together, and ordered the chairman to carry them both away; perfectly representing, both in love and nakedness, and want of eyes to see that they were naked, our first happy parents. Sunday last I had the pleasure of hearing the whole from the lady's own mouth."

This letter was written in March, 1712, when Lady Mary was in her 22nd year. Five months afterwards she "scuttled away (as she phrases it) to be married to Mr Montagu;" that is to say, her father was against the match, and herself not much for it; only she thought a handsome young gentleman better than a dictatorial parent.

On this spot, too, resided Horace Walpole. Almost all his town letters are dated from Arlington-street, before he went to live in Berkeley Square. It is here and at Strawberry Hill that he wrote, and jested, and was visited by his friends Conway, Selwyn, and Gray, during the happiest period of his life. (Fancy you see Gray turning the corner, with his delicate, thoughtful, and perhaps somewhat fastidious aspect). We shall say more of

Horace Walpole when we come to the close of his life; but we must not omit to mention that in the year 1771, an extraordinary circumstance took place in his house in this street. It was broken open "without his servants being alarmed; all the locks were forced off his drawers, cabinets, &c., and their contents scattered about the room, and yet nothing was taken away."—So says his editor, Lord Dover. Walpole says nothing. He never even alludes to the circumstance. Lord Dover tells us, that Walpole's Parisian correspondent, the celebrated Madame du Deffand, attributed it to a suspicion entertained of his being in correspondence with the Duc de Choiseul, the late French minister. French affairs were at that time in a desperate state under Louis the Fifteenth and Madame du Barry. They puzzled the English Government; and there was a talk of war. We suspect Madame du Deffand was right; or at least that Choiseul's affairs had to do with the matter; for it appears doubtful, by a preceding note of Lord Dover's, whether his Lordship was right in saying that nothing had been taken away. A letter written by Madame du Deffand in the preceding December, and "filled with details relative to the Duc de Choiseul," is, he tells us, "unfortunately lost." Walpole, for reasons best known to himself, may have given out that nothing was taken away; but the loss of the letter may account for the scattered papers. Walpole had been in Paris a few years before; he was in constant correspondence with the place; he went there again a few months after the violation of his cabinets; and he always busied himself in secret history.

Imagine the attempt to commit such an outrage *now!*

CHAPTER VIII.

ST. JAMES'S-STREET AND THE CLUBS—WILBERFORCE'S FIRST APPEARANCE IN A SUBSCRIPTION-HOUSE.—PITT AND FOX. — HESSE AND ADAIR. — STORY OF MR PORTER; THE TYING OF THE SHOE.—BUTLER ON GAMING.—COLONEL BLOOD.—GIBBON.—CLASSICAL MEMORIES ASSOCIATED WITH THE DISTRICT OF ST JAMES'S.—DISAPPEARANCE OF KELLY'S SALOON, ANGERSTEIN'S GALLERY, AND CARLTON HOUSE.— MICHAEL KELLY, AND HIS EXAMINATION BEFORE THE COMMISSIONERS OF THE INCOME TAX.—ADDISON'S MODE OF LIFE.—SUICIDES OF CAREY AND BUDGELL.

IF disreputable men, at the period when the events recorded in the latter part of the preceding chapter occurred, found it difficult to get into a single club, others of a different sort were often members of several clubs at a time. This was the case with Wilberforce on his entering the world. We will quote his own account of his first appearance in these establishments, as affording a good abstract idea of the thing called a subscription-house. The date of the account is about sixty years since; but with exceptions as to the more sober attractions of club-houses on newer principles, it will apply still.

"When I left the university," says he, "so little did I know of general society, that I came up to London stored with arguments to prove the authenticity of Rowley's poems; and now I was at once immersed in politics and fashion. The very first time I went to Boodle's, I won twenty-five guineas of the Duke of Norfolk. I belonged at this time to five clubs—Miles and Evans's, Brookes's, Boodle's, White's, Goostree's. The first time I was at Brookes's, scarcely knowing any one, I joined, from mere shyness, in play at the faro table, where George Selwyn kept bank. A friend who knew my inexperience, and regarded me as a victim decked out for sacrifice, called to me, 'What, Wilberforce! is that you?' Selwyn quite resented the interference; and turning to him said, in his most expressive tone, ' O, Sir, don't interrupt Mr Wilberforce; he could not be better employed!' Nothing could be more luxurious than the style of these clubs. Fox, Sheridan, Fitzpatrick, and all your leading men frequented them, and associated upon the easiest terms; you chatted, played at cards, or gambled as you pleased. I was one of those who met to spend an evening in memory of Shakspeare, at the Boar's-head, Eastcheap. Many professed wits were present, but Pitt was the most amusing of the party. We played a good deal at Goostree's; and I well remember the intense earnestness he displayed when joining in those games of chance. He perceived their increasing fascination, and soon after suddenly abandoned them for ever."

Pitt left the gaming-table for gambling of a

more awful kind. He played at the game of war with the blood and money of nations, and broke his heart on his last stake; as the conqueror himself did afterwards. Pitt's "intense earnestness" was but an evidence of one and the same passion for excitement and victory. Great public interests tend to carry such men into the greatest field of action, especially if they have not many counteracting tendencies. Pitt was all bone and will: he had not the flesh and blood of Fox. Fox is said to have remarked, that the deepest play he ever knew was between the year 1772 and the beginning of the American war. It was not a great time, either for war like the one that succeeded it, or for the nobler aspirations that distinguish the present. It was the fag-end of a reasonable and comfortable time enough, with luxurious philosophers and historians, all sedentary; and its greatest wits were identical with the greatest gossips. Hume, Gibbon, Walpole, and Selwyn, will supply the names. Fox gave as an instance of what he said, that five thousand pounds were staked on a single card at faro.

Depth of play, however, is not always to be estimated by absolute pecuniary amount. A relative nine-and-twopence may ruin a costermonger; and desperate wretches of a higher rank, in staking their last guinea, have been far greater losers than fools who risked their five thousand. Savages have staked their wives and children; and, indeed, what else has been done by hundreds of well-dressed savages at White's and Crockford's? Adair, the surgeon, who, about a dozen years before the date of the above gambling epoch, married into the family of Lord Albemarle, had a friend in the Army Pay-office, a Mr Hesse, who so completely ruined a small fortune, that he committed suicide in consequence, and drove his wife mad; a state from which she was ultimately rescued by the good surgeon, who had taken her into his own house. (How consolatory it is, by the side of such horrors, to be able to record such virtues!)

The most inveterate, though not most tragical, instance we can call to mind of infatuation for the gaming-table (for the victim appears to have been a bachelor) is recorded in the same curious work which has supplied us with the preceding anecdote, the *Loungers' Common-place Book.* The author has told the story so well, and his work, upon the whole, is so little known, that we shall repeat it in his own words.

A Mr Porter, he tells us, in the reign of Queen Anne, possessed one of the best estates in the county of Northumberland, the fee of which, in less than twelve months, he lost at hazard.

The last night of his career, when he had just perfected the wicked work, and was stepping down-stairs to throw himself into his carriage, which waited at the door of a well-known house, he suddenly went back into the room where his "friends" were assembled, and insisted that the person he had been playing with should give him one chance of recovery, or fight with him. His rational proposition was this :—that his carriage, the trinkets and loose money in his pocket, his town house, plate, and furniture, should be valued in a lump, at a certain sum, and be thrown for at a single cast. No persuasions could prevail on him to depart from his purpose. He threw; and conducting the winner to the door, told the coachman *that* was his master, and heroically marched forth without house, home, or any one creditable source of support.

He retired to an obscure lodging in a cheap part of the town, subsisting partly on charity, sometimes acting as the substitute of a marker at a billiard-table, and occasionally as helper at a livery stable.

In this miserable condition, with nakedness

and famine staring him in the face, exposed to the taunts and insults of those whom he had once supported, he was recognised by an old friend, who gave him ten guineas to purchase necessaries.

He expended five in procuring decent apparel; with the other five he repaired to a common gaming-house, and increased them to fifty; he then adjourned to White's, sat down with his former associates, and won twenty thousand pounds. Returning the next night, he lost it all, and after subsisting many years in abject and sordid penury, died, a ragged beggar, at a penny lodging-house in St Giles's.

Had he, concludes his historian, fractured his leg on quitting the gaming-house with twenty thousand pounds, or been doomed, by a *lettre de cachet*, to straw, bread and water, and a shaved head, for six months, in a dark room, it might have brought him to his senses, and have prevented so ignominious a relapse.

This is doubtful. What is bred in the dice, will seldom come out of the dice-box. If starvation, insult, and ingratitude could not cure such a man, why should a fractured leg, or the desperation of a dark room? Nor was this wretch perhaps much unhappier while a beggar than he was before. The hope of a shilling would be as stirring a thing to him as that of fifty guineas in his higher condition, and the misery of losing it as full of sensation. And he probably gambled for the shilling upon a tub turned upside down. What he desired was excitement, not respectability or reflection. Gamblers are drunkards. What care they for wives, children, friends, appearances, decency, or anything else, except perhaps the last closing sensation when it comes, so long as the blood spins round, and they can laugh or curse to their hearts content?

But enough of the tragedy of this folly. The best bit of comedy we ever heard in connexion with it, was the famous sentence addressed by a losing gamester to an unlucky urchin who happened to be stooping down, tying his shoe. The gamester had just issued out of his White's or Brookes's in anything but a benevolent state of mind, when observing a boy in this provoking state of reasonable occupation, he put his foot against his unsuspecting body, and sent him pitching across the street with the following voluminous remark :—" You are *always* tying that shoe ! "

If argument could have done anything with gamblers, exquisite Butler would have supplied it, in some of his happiest wit :—

> " What fool would trouble Fortune more,
> When she has been too kind before,
> Or tempt her to take back again
> What she had thrown away in vain,
> By idly venturing her good graces
> To be disposed of by ames-aces ;
> Or settling it in trusts and uses
> Out of his power, on trays and deuces :
> To put it to the chance, and try,

I' the ballot of a box and die,
Whether his money be his own,
And lose it, if he be o'erthrown;
As if he were betray'd and set
By his own stars to every cheat,
Or wretchedly condemn'd by Fate
To throw dice for his own estate!"

But we must conclude our account of Saint James's-street by hastily noticing two circumstances, of very different interest from one another: first, that it was in this street, as Mr Smith observes, and not in Piccadilly, that Blood, who attempted to steal the crown, attacked the Duke of Ormond in his coach with the intention of bearing him off to Tyburn and hanging him; and that in the house numbered 76, at the corner of Little St James's-street, then the property of Elmsley the bookseller, died the sedentary and luxurious Gibbon; the most exact and most entertaining, if not the most ingenuous of historians.

The whole district extending eastward from

the Green Park to the Haymarket, and southward from Piccadilly to St James's Park, having St James's Square for its centre, accords with the better part of the reputation of St James's-street, and is classical as well as courtly ground. In St James's Place lived Rogers, and once lived Addison. In St James's Market Mrs Oldfield, then a girl, was found by "Captain Farquhar," in a tavern kept by an aunt, giving promise of her genius for the stage by reciting plays to her friends. In Cleveland-row lived Selwyn, and some years since the Duke of Sutherland, famous (as Marquis of Stafford) for his gallery of pictures. In Bury-street Steele resided during one of his honeymoons. In Jermyn-street Shenstone used to lodge when he came to town; and there, also, at the St James's Hotel, Sir Walter Scott, returning from Italy, rested on his way to die at Abbotsford. In Charles-street once resided Lord Byron. In York-street the

Wedgewoods (the friends of Coleridge) set up their manufactory of Etruscan ware, which introduced a classical taste into half the tea-tables of England. In St James's Square lived Lord Bathurst (the friend of Pope), Bishop Louth, Francis (the supposed author of "Junius"), and we know not for what period or in whose house, probably that of Lord Bathurst, Martha Blount, who was here visited by the poet. Finally, in Pall-Mall we have Sydenham, De Foe, Gainsborough, Windham, Sir Charles Bunbury, Gay (walking), all his friends no doubt (both walking and talking), all the accomplished visitors at the mansion of the Temples; those at Marlborough House, particularly Steele and Addison; at Bubb Doddington's, including Thomson and Cumberland; at Carlton House, including Fox, Sheridan (who at one time lived next door to it), and Walter Scott; all the Opera people who once thronged through Kelly's Saloon;

and now we have the principal clubs on the new, though not on the newest, principles (the *Whittington* being *that*, and an admirable one it is, and one of the greatest signs of the times. Mr Douglas Jerrold was fortunate in inducing the east end of the town to set so high and truly polite an example to the west).

Some of these houses have vanished, both small and great. Poor Kelly's Saloon has gone; over which, when the musician commenced wine-merchant, Sheridan's wicked wit proposed to inscribe " Michael Kelly, Composer of Wine, and Importer of Music." Angerstein's house has gone, where that princely merchant, with his fine taste, made the collection of pictures which was the germ of the National Gallery, and which has not been borne out as worthily as it might have been, by some of its fruit. Carlton House has gone, with its (upon the whole, in spite of Fox and others) flimsy taste and flustered pretensions to liberality, coolly dropped when the prince came to be the monarch. This palace, which stood back from the street on the site of the memorial erected to the Duke of York, had a screen of columns that supported nothing; which is said to have given rise to the following couplet, probably written by some opera poet whose Italian recollections it disconcerted:—

> Care colonne, che fate quà?
> Non sappiamo, in verità.
>
> Dear little columns, how came you so?
> Why, to say truth, we really don't know.

Kelly's Saloon was at the corner of St Alban's-street, and communicated with the Opera House, of which he was manager. He was a jovial, good-natured man, a composer of taste, and was not without popularity as a singer, though he had a poor, sharp voice. He made quite a " sensation " with poor Mrs Crouch, then a beautiful woman and charming singer, in the duet of " Oh, thou wert born to please me." He was in love with her. He was author of "When pensive I thought of my love," and other pleasing airs, including the march in *Bluebeard*. But his managements of all sorts came to nothing, as the reader may conclude from the following entertaining passage in his Memoirs. The narrative was probably "cooked up" by Theodore Hook, his amanuensis in the work; but the spirit of the thing is the man all over. It is a scene between Mr Kelly and the Commissioners of the Income-tax:—

"So, Mr Kelly," said one of the Commissioners, "you have returned your income to us at £500. You must have a very mean opinion of our understandings, Sir, to think that you could induce us to receive such a return; when we are aware that your income, from your various professional engagements, must amount to twice or thrice that sum."

"Sir," said Mr Kelly, "I am free to confess I have erred in my return; but vanity is the cause, and vanity is the badge of all my tribe. I have returned myself as having £500 per annum, when, in fact, I have not 500 pence of certain income."

"Pray, Sir," asked the Commissioner, "are you not stage-manager at the Opera-House?"

"Yes, Sir," answered Mr Kelly, "but there is not even a nominal salary attached to that office. I perform its duties to gratify my love of music."

"Well, but, Mr Kelly," continued the examiner, "you teach?"

"I do, Sir," replied Mr Kelly; "but I have no pupils."

"I think," observed another gentleman, who had not before spoken, "that you are an oratorio and concert singer?"

"You are quite right," said Mr Kelly to his new antagonist; "but I have no engagement."

"Well, but at all events," remarked Mr Kelly's first inquisitor, "you have a very good salary at Drury-lane?"

"A very good one, indeed, Sir," answered Mr Kelly; "but then it is never paid."

"You have always a fine benefit, Sir," said the other, who seemed to know something of theatricals.

"Always, Sir," was Mr Kelly's reply; "but the expenses attending it are very great; and whatever profit remains after defraying them, is mortgaged to liquidate debts incurred by building my saloon. The fact is, Sir, I am at present very like St George's Hospital, supported by voluntary contributions."

The Commissioners laughed, and the return was allowed to pass.

But before we conclude our survey of Pall-Mall, and glance into Carlton Gardens, we must look back a little at Addison, and others. Addison's mode of life, during his residence in

St James's Place, has been described by Johnson, on the authority of Pope. "He had in the house with him Budgell, and perhaps Philips. His chief companions were Steele, Budgell, Philips, Carey, Davenant, and Colonel Brett, with one or other of whom he always breakfasted. He studied all the morning; then dined at a tavern, and went afterwards to Button's. From the coffee-house he went again to the tavern, where he often sat too late, and drank too much wine."

By "having Budgell or Philips in the house with him," is meant, we suppose, that Addison gave them apartments in order to be secure of their society. Budgell, who was his second-cousin and probably his amanuensis, and who committed suicide, sometimes wrote in the *Spectator*. Philips was Ambrose Philips the pastoral writer, whose nursery effusions were unduly depreciated, in consequence of their being a little overdone. Carey was an Oxford man, who contributed to the *Spectator*. Budgell was a man of wayward temper and violent passions, who, besides getting his affairs into disorder, quarrelled with everybody, and seems to have thrown away the best opportunities. Pope has given celebrity to a charge made against him, of forging the will of Dr Tindal, who left him £2000 to the exclusion of his nephew, the historian.

> " Let Budgell charge low Grub-street on my quill,
> And write whate'er he please,—except my will."

Budgell's final misfortune seems to have been, that he left himself no friend to open his mind to ; or at least, that he gave no friend credit enough for being worth the confidence. He was a man of considerable wit and ability, and might have been saved by having a little more faith. Davenant was Charles Davenant, the political writer, son of Sir William : and Colonel Brett was the gay gentleman about town, who "married Savage's mother and bought Cibber's wig." All these gentlemen, therefore, may be looked upon as frequenters of St James's Place. The assemblage, upon the whole, is a curious one for Addison's table. It shows that he was not quite so nice in his company as in his writings; but then it is to be considered that we could not well have had the writings without the company. It should be added, as an excuse for the too much wine which Addison drank at the tavern, that he was a man of unhealthy blood; in this respect resembling his cousin Budgell.

CHAPTER IX.

ABODE OF MR ROGERS.—WARREN HASTINGS, AND OTHER RESIDENTS IN ST JAMES'S PLACE.—CLEVELAND ROW AND THE DUCHESS OF CLEVELAND.—SIR RICHARD STEELE AND HIS WIFE.—HORACE WALPOLE AT A FIRE.—JERMYN, EARL OF ST ALBANS.—CHARACTER OF CHARLES, FOURTEENTH DUKE OF NORFOLK.—END OF LORD CASTLEREAGH.—NELL GWYN.—HOUSE BUILT BY ATHENIAN STUART.—COUNTESS OF LOVELACE.—SIR CHARLES GRANDISON.—LONDON LIBRARY.—JOHNSON AND SAVAGE.—SIR ROBERT WALPOLE AND MARLBOROUGH HOUSE.

MR ROGERS, with a felicity rare in a poet's lot, had the good fortune, in his house in St James's Place, to be able to exemplify the taste which he evinced in such matters in his "Epistle to a Friend." Mr Smith informs us, that it was even built for him; and several writers have recorded the elegance of the interior, of its pictures and prints, the chimney-pieces designed by Flaxman, and the cabinets decorated by Stothard. The house too is pitched, just as a poet might desire, in one of the quietest nooks of an elegant quarter, with a park in front of it and London at the back; so that he might turn to country or town as the mood inclined him. It was pleasant to see house and inmate so well suited. It is consolatory, at the same time, to reflect, that if Mr Rogers had been unable to possess so charming an abode, he was poet enough to have made a good case out of an humbler one. The only thing to be regretted in the lots of poets is when they are enabled to possess neither real nor ideal elegancies in peace, but must have their fairy palaces crushed by the rudest heels of necessity.

In St James's Place lived Warren Hastings,

and Henry Grattan. Wilkes also had lodgings there; and at No. 13 resided poor Mrs Robinson, who fancied that to be a Prince's mistress was to be loved for life. She had probably indulged in a consequent tone of exaction, not calculated to lengthen the dream.

Cleveland Row derives its ignoble name from the "beautiful fury," Barbara Villiers, Duchess of Cleveland, so made by Charles the Second, whose mistress she became the first day of the "Blessed Restoration," and whose mistress she continued to be (among others) during his whole reign, not by reason of her continued delightfulness, but of his Sacred Majesty's fear of her scolding and violence. She often put him in such a flustered state of mind, that he could not conceal it at the council board. Her life was one selfish round of incontinence of every sort, worthily closed by such a dropsy as destroyed all her beauty and rendered her a sight. She appears to have felt so little for other people, that it provokes one to feel nothing for herself. We shall have to pay her our disrespects again when we come to Whitehall.

Here follow two letters of Steele's in connexion with Bury-street; the first addressed to the wife above alluded to just before his wedding-day; the second to her mother. His addressing the former as "wife," by anticipation, is quite in the style of his fine turn of gallantry, which combined the extremes of respect and passion.

"To Mrs Scurlock.*

"October 8, 1707.

"My dear Wife,—You were not, I am sure, awake so soon as I was for you, and

* It was the custom at that time to address an unmarried young lady as "Mrs," though in general with the addition of

desired the blessing of God upon you. After that first duty, my next is to let you know I am in health this morning, which I know you are solicitous for. I believe it would not be amiss if, some time this afternoon, you took a coach or chair, and went to see a house next door to Lady Buckley's, towards St James's Street, which is to be let. I have a solid reason for quickening my diligence in all affairs of the world, which is, that you may partake in them, and will make me labour more than any incitation of ambition or wealth could do. After I have implored the help of Providence, I will have no motive to my actions but the love of the best creature living, to whom I am an obedient husband."

her Christian name. The title of "Miss," which is an abbreviation of "Mistress," originally implied a familiarity not of the most respectful kind, and had hardly yet made its way into good company.

"To Mrs Scurlock, Sen.

October 14, 1707.

"Honoured Mother, I am very sorry to find, by Mrs Scurlock's letter, that you keep your bed, which makes me almost in despair of seeing you so soon as I promised myself.

"I have taken an house in Bury-street, St James's, and beg your leave to remove your goods thither; where I hope we shall all live together in the strictest love and friendship. Whatever better prospects your daughter might well have given herself, from her great merit and good qualities, I shall take care to have it said that she could not have married more advantageously with regard to her mother, who shall always find me her most obedient son, and most humble servant.

"Your daughter gives her duty to you."

Steele injured his fortunes by a curious

mixture of complexional carelessness with a patriotic sense of duty; and his wife, under the inconveniences to which this subjected her, was unfortunately not of a temperament warm enough to substitute caresses for remonstrance. But she did not want sense otherwise: she had an abundance of respectable qualities; and as Steele was always a gentleman and a man of gallantry, even towards his wife, they got on as well together as most married couples, perhaps better; certainly better than his staider friend Addison with the Countess of Warwick. Steele should have married the lively Countess, and Addison the sober "Prue," and then neither Sir Richard would have wanted money, nor the illustrious Joseph repose.

In Bury-street Horace Walpole might once have been seen standing in the snow, in an embroidered suit, at five o'clock in the morning! So strange may a natural proceeding appear, when isolated from its circumstances.

"I am at present," says he in one of his letters, "confined with a cold which I caught by going to a fire in the middle of the night, and in the middle of the snow, two days ago. About five in the morning Harry waked me with a candle in his hand, and cried, 'Pray, your Honour, don't be frightened!'—'No, Harry, I am not; but what is it that I am not to be frightened at?'—'There is a great fire here in St James's-street.'—I rose, and indeed thought all St James's-street was on fire, but it proved in Bury-street. However, you know I can't resist going to a fire; for it is certainly the only horrid sight that is fine. I slipped on my slippers and an embroidered suit that hung on the chair, and ran to Bury-street, and stepped into a pipe that was broken up for water. It would have made a picture — the horror of the flames, the snow, the day breaking with difficulty through so foul a night, and my figure, *party per pale*,* mud and gold. It put me in mind of Lady Margaret Herbert's providence, who asked somebody for a *pretty* pattern for a nightcap. 'Lord!' said they, 'what signifies the pattern of a nightcap?' 'Oh! child,' said she, 'but, you know, in case of fire.'"

Some tragical circumstances follow, which do not so well fall in with the embroidery and the slippers. Walpole laughs at the fine nightcap; but it is pretty evident he thought fit to dress his own person for the occasion, that he might not appear to a disadvantage in his reader's imagination. At least, this is the impression produced by his constantly talking of such matters.

We know not what occasioned the name of Bury-street. Charles the Second and his brother James gave rise to King-street, Duke-

* *Part per pale* is a term in heraldry, to express division in stripes.

street, Charles-street, York-street, and St James's church. York-street is said to have been the first street in London that was paved. Jermyn-street and St Alban's-street were christened from Henry Jermyn, Earl of St Alban's, who figures in Grammont, and who is understood to have been secretly married to Queen Henrietta Maria, widow of Charles the First. He is said to have ruled her as arbitrarily as she ruled the King. Jermyn lived in a mansion on the site of the present Norfolk House, in which George the Third was born; and in this house, in the year 1815, died Charles, Duke of Norfolk, a pretended liberalist and gross man of the world, huge and fat, who looked like a grazier. The Duke passed his time ludicrously enough between aristocratic hauteur and affected love of liberty, between the vulgarest excesses and pretensions to taste and knowledge. He was an enormous eater and drinker, and grossly negligent in his person.

He died immensely rich, without leaving a penny (so to speak) to his oldest friends, and entirely overlooking poor Captain Morris, the song-writer, who had been his companion for many years, and whom he detained for hours with him on his very death-bed, in order that a better heart than his own might solace him to the last. He acted much in the same manner to his natural children, of whom he had multitudes. These are the reasons we speak as plainly about him as we do.

The official residence of the Bishop of London is next door to Norfolk House.

Poor Lord Castlereagh, an unpopular and bad minister, but not an ungenerous or unsuffering man, had his town-house in St James's Square, the one now occupied by the Military and Naval Club. He was accidentally watched out of it the day before he killed himself, and followed up Pall Mall and St James's-street into Piccadilly, by a gentleman to whom he was pointed out, and who was surprised to see him buy a penknife of a Jew-boy by the White Horse Cellar. This was the fatal instrument. He lay "in state" (what a state !) in his house in the Square; and when his coffin was taken out of the hearse at the door of Westminster Abbey, the exulting shouts of the populace were heard by the mourners in the interior. What a sound to fall on their ears ! It was a savage exhibition of feeling; but it must be added, that Tory arrogance and violence had taught it. Society is now beginning to understand its decencies better on all sides; and Toryism itself is descending into its grave, if with no sorrow on the part of the spectators, yet not without something like a wondering pity.

In a house in the south-west corner of the Square and stretching into Pall Mall, lived and died Nell Gwyn, the least respectable in one sense, but far most respectable in others, of all the mistresses of Charles the Second, for she was faithful to him and good-hearted. Wishing to give some money one day in this house at a concert, she is said to have turned round to the King and asked him to supply her. His Majesty declared he had not a guinea about him; and the Duke of York, his brother (James II.), on being applied to, made the same answer; upon which exclaimed Nell, "Bless me! what company I have got into!" Pennant says, that "within memory" the back room on the ground floor of this house was entirely of looking-glass. Tillotson got into trouble by preaching Nelly's funeral sermon and recording her charities, on the strength of her being a penitent; but good Queen Mary (consort of William III.) had courage enough to defend him.

The house once occupied by Lord Ellenborough, the chief-justice, among those in the north-west corner, and easily distinguished by its architectural elegance, was built by the artist known by the name of Athenian Stuart (for his journey to and publications on Athens). If our memory does not deceive us, it is not unlike a house in Florence built by the divine hand of Raphael.

Not far from this house to the right, on the north-west side of the Square, resided a poet's daughter (worthy of that title, by all accounts, for the vivacity and liberality of her spirit)— the Countess of Lovelace (Ada Byron). The noble Earl her husband is related to the family of Locke. It is pleasant to think that her Ladyship had so pretty a title matrimonial. Lovelace is the name of one of the most elegant of our old poets; not so great a one as her father, but truly deserving the epithet; and he was of a noble family to boot. Richardson gave the name of Lovelace to the gay reprobate in *Clarissa ;* and this reminds us that in St James's Square he has placed the abode of another hero of his—Sir Charles Grandison, the pink of impossible proprieties. Richardson's Lovelace is a scoundrel, who nevertheless recognises the existence of something better than himself; if, indeed, he is not a mere inconsistent exhibition of one kind of power in nature, contesting for ascendancy with another. And even the divine Clarissa has more of the love of will and power in her than she suspects. But Grandison manifestly sees nothing below the moon more lovely than himself. He is eternally contemplating himself in the glass of his perfections, and is made a master of the art of duelling in order that he may be sure of conquering his man without killing him, and so secure the united good opinions of God and the West End.

We must not take leave of St James's Square without expressing our constant sense of the merits and utility of the institution some years since founded under the title of the London Library. It has transferred itself to this place from Pall Mall, and is situated between the houses just mentioned and next door to the Windham Club. It is the only great collection of the kind which allows subscribers to have books at their own houses. The collection is excellent, the subscription cheap, and the attendance urbane. Readers disappointed in circulating libraries can there get books of the highest reputation in all languages, and enjoy or turn them to account at their own firesides— an incalculable advantage to most people, but especially to authors not in good health. If it were not for the London Library, the writer of these remarks on the Streets would be forced to omit a considerable portion of whatsoever the good-natured reader may find in them to amuse him.

Authorship has yet another memorandum to make on this Square, not altogether so pleasant. Johnson and Savage once paced it all night, for want of money to procure a lodging. They did it, however, in no sneaking state of mind.

They were gallant partisans, brimful of zeal against the minister (Walpole); and as they tramped hungrily along, were resolved, as Johnson said, "to stand by their country." Johnson's after life, in point of industry and courage, was a magnanimous comment on this incident. Savage failed for dishonesty. Still he had points in his history worthy of commiseration. At this juncture, perhaps, his integrity had not given way; and the two men were strongly and interestingly brought together by a mutual bond of intellect and want. Walpole probably resided in the neighbourhood. He possessed at one time a house at the corner of Pall Mall, by Marlborough House; and. at another he resided in Cleveland Row, where the personal scuffle is said to have taken place between him and Lord Townsend, which is ridiculed in the *Beggar's Opera* in the persons of Locket and Peachum.

Walpole is said to have bought the house in

Pall Mall, in order to spite the old Duchess of Marlborough, who wished to make a way from her premises into that street, which the statesman's purchase frustrated. The grounds of Marlborough House were an offset from the park, given to the Duke by Queen Anne, when the house was built by the nation. It remained in the occupation of the family, till it became the residence of the present King of the Belgians; and afterwards that of the Queen Dowager.

CHAPTER X.

PALL MALL AND THE GAME FROM WHICH ITS NAME IS DE-
RIVED.—SCHOMBERG HOUSE AND GAINSBOROUGH.—JEW-
ISH SYNAGOGUE. — THE SONGS OF ZION. — MUSICAL
CHARACTER OF THE JEWS.—ASSASSINATION OF THYNNE.—
PERSONS CONCERNED IN THIS TRANSACTION, KÖNINGS-
MARK, CAPTAIN VRATZ, LIEUTENANT STERN, AND BOROSKY
THE POLE. — BUBB DODDINGTON.—HIS CHARACTER AND
HISTORY.—CUMBERLAND'S AMUSING ACCOUNT OF HIM.

PALL MALL, as late as the times of Charles the Second, was a walk between trees and the Park; and it took its name from the favourite recreation of that monarch, who probably found the soil fitter for it than that of the walk in the Park, still known by part of its appellation, the Mall. The ground was a little higher. In neither place, however, does the game appear to have realised its best possible locality.

"I walked," said Pepys, "in the Park, discoursing with the keeper of the Pell Mell, who was sweeping it; who told me of what the earth is mixed that do floor the *Mall*, and that over all there is cockle-shell powdered, and spread to keep it fast; which however, in dry weather, turns to dust and deads the ball."

This game was brought out of France. Pall Mall, Pail Mail, Pell Mell, in French *Pale maille*, in Italian *Palamaglia*, is defined by Florio, in his old Italian and English dictionary, to be "a tough ashen stick with a mallet, hollow at both ends, fastened at one end of the stick, to strike, to hit, and to cast a round bowl made of box-wood, much used in Italy and France among gentlemen." The ball was driven at a distance through an iron hoop. Pall was the ball, and Mall the stick. The word is retained in the Maul-stick of the painters. We shall have more to say on this recreation when we come to the Park.

The tall old red brick house, No. 80, formerly occupied by Messrs Payne and Foss, was originally called Schomberg House, having been built for the Duke of Schomberg, who died in the service of William the Third in Ireland. It was subsequently in the occupation of the Holdernesse family, and then was divided, some say rebuilt, into three separate abodes by "Jack Astley," the painter, who, marrying a widow of fortune, retired from his profession. Jack, who was a dashing fellow, and wooed and married in the course of ten days, lived in the centre house, which was afterwards occupied by another fashionable portrait-painter, Cosway; then by Dr Graham, the quack, who made a sensation with his mud baths and his elastic beds; and the house next to this, westward, is worth looking at, as being the residence of a genuine artist, Gainsborough. His fine free natural powers as a landscape painter are well known to the visitors of the National Gallery; and he is said to have given Sir Joshua some uneasiness as a portrait painter. He was a good-natured, restless man, full of impulse, the friend of Sterne and Garrick, and passionately fond of music. Smith, the Antiquarian Rambler, and biographer of Nollekens, went while a boy to visit him in company with that sculptor, and found him listening in ecstasy to a Colonel Hamilton, who was playing the violin, and who had long wanted a picture of his. Gainsborough held up his finger to Nollekens as they came in, by way of requesting him to maintain the silence; and on Hamilton's leaving off, he said, "Now, my dear Colonel, if you will but go on, I will give you that picture of the Boy on the Stile, which you have so often wished to purchase of me." (There is an engraving of it by a pupil of Woollett.) The Colonel went on with his performance, and, at the conclusion, went off with the picture. The painter, who had been modelling an ass's head, then turned to Smith, and said, "You enjoyed the music, my little fellow, and I am sure you long for this model. There, I will give it you." He did; and Smith went off with the model.

It was this true overflowing-hearted child of Nature (and Nature loves such children, and is sure to reward them somehow) who said, in the delirium of his last moments, "We are all going to heaven, and Vandyke is of the party."

When we spoke of St Alban's-street, at the corner of which poor harmless Kelly had his saloon, we ought to have observed that the name and the street itself (as far as horseway is concerned) have disappeared, the only passage remaining being now the west portion of the Arcade of the Opera House. "Opera *Ar*cade" is its appellation;—a vile cacophony, unendurable to Italian ears.

The name "St Alban's" is retained in the upper portion of this thoroughfare, where it crosses Charles-street and becomes St Alban's Place: a spot in which many of our readers may be surprised to hear there is a Jewish synagogue. People seldom think of Jews, except in connection with the City; forgetting, that the wealth which they get in the City makes them denizens of the West End and lords of the world. "Money," said the wise man, "is the sinews of war;" and next door to Apsley House lives a Rothschild. A visit to the Synagogue on one of its high days is a thing of no little interest. We there see the oldest known worship existing, except that of the Parsees. It is affecting to hear the "Songs of Zion" in their own language (or what at least is the nearest to it), and to see the Law of Moses brought forth from the "Tabernacle," and held up to the reverent gaze of the Children of Israel. Roman Catholics are not the monopolisers which they slyly pretend to be, of all the

> Pride, pomp, and circumstance of glorious *worship*.

Nor have they always the best singing. The singing in these synagogues is often beautiful; and curiously enough, a Jewish place of worship is more in harmony with the neighbourhood of an opera house than many a fashionable Protestant Church. The Jews are still the musical people they were of old. You can hardly, indeed, mention the name of a celebrated living composer, not an Italian, but somebody will be ready to swear he is a Jew. Nay, there are several Italian singers asserted to be Jews, not excepting Pasta; and as the new Pope is so good a Christian that many of the old Papists insist he is no Christian at all, perhaps they will discover that he also is a Jew. There was certainly one Jew (not to speak it lightly) whom he more resembles than any prince who has yet sat on the Papal throne.

But to return to Pall Mall. At the corner of this gentle spot (the arcade leading from St Alban's Place) there occurred, in the reign of Charles the Second, one of the most extraordinary outrages that ever astonished a civilised country. This was the famous assassination, on a Sunday evening in February, no later than eight o'clock, of a man of family and fortune of the name of Thynne, as he was returning in his carriage from a house in St James's-street. He was shot with a blunderbuss; and the assassins, for a moment, escaped. They were three foreigners—a Swede, a German, and a Pole; and their instigator, without a doubt, was another foreigner, a Swedish Count, Köningsmark, who had designs on an heiress to whom Thynne was contracted. The men were his retainers. The discharger of the blunderbuss had slept in his house the night before; and both this man (Borosky), who was his servant, and the German, who was a Lieutenant of the name of Stern, confessed that they believed the Count to be at the bottom of the murder; but as the Swede, a Captain Vratz, had taken the direction of it on himself, and stubbornly refused to criminate his employer, the tools were hung, and the principal acquitted. The fact is, that Thynne had left the court interest to join that of Monmouth, and oppose the succession of the Duke of York; and there is reason to believe that the King and judges were bent on getting him off. Thynne, who appears to have had better friends than he deserved, and in resentment of whose death (not unmixed perhaps with some other grounds of irritation against Köningsmark) Lord Cavendish, afterwards first Duke of Devonshire, with the chivalrous gallantry of his race, endeavoured to make the villain fight him, had a monument erected to his memory in Westminster Abbey, on which the particulars of the murder are sculptured, and which still amazes, or amuses, the spectator; as though there had been a virtue in being assassinated. But it was done to vex the Court. The mourners intended also a pompous epitaph, recording the virtues of the great rich man and the meritorious amount of slugs which had entered his body; but the Dean (Sprat, the servile Bishop of Rochester) was too glad to see it furnish its own grounds for rejection, in its ridiculous language as well as its party politics.

It is not a little remarkable that something strange is attached to the history or character of every one of the persons concerned in this transaction.

Thynne (from a cousin of whom is descended the Marquis of Bath) was called Tom of Ten Thousand, on account of his wealth. In order to increase this wealth by union with an heiress, he is said to have forsaken a lady whom he had seduced under promise of marriage; and this circumstance occasioned some verses to the following purport :—

> Tom of Ten Thousand, of Lougleat Hall,
> In his days would have never miscarried,
> Had he married the woman he lived withal,
> Or lived with the woman he married.

If we are to judge from the name of "Issachar" given him by Dryden, he was a silly spendthrift.

The lady to whom this luckless man of prosperity was contracted, was a girl of fifteen, who was already the widow of another nominal husband—Lord Ogle (a Cavendish), son of the second Duke of Newcastle. She was heiress of the house of Percy; and appears to have cared neither for Thynne nor Köningsmark; for within four months after the former's death she took for her third husband the Proud Duke of Somerset (as he was afterwards called). It was she of whom he spoke, when, in reproof of his second Duchess, who had playfully set herself on his knee, the stupid fellow said, "My first wife, madam, was a Percy; yet she never took such a liberty."

Köningsmark, who was himself only twenty-three years of age, was one of those victims of pride of birth, who, agreeably to the wretched continental educations then furnished to men of military breeding, placed all virtue in "blood." He thought any shame was to be wiped out by a gallant action in the field. He said so; and perhaps perished in consequence, for he died in battle four years after the commission of his crime. The popular belief that he was the same Count Köningsmark that was the victim of an alleged intrigue with the consort of George the First, has long been proved to be unfounded. The latter was his brother.

Captain Vratz, the Count's chief instrument, appears to have held the like brutal notions of gentility, graced (if grace it can be called) with the injured virtue of "fidelity to his employer." He refused to implicate him by a syllable; said he had taken his friend's quarrel with Thynne upon himself; ridiculously pretended he had a right to shoot Thynne for refusing to answer a challenge he had sent him "by the post;" though he did not think it genteel to do it with his own hand; and when he was told of the bad chance he stood in the next world as well as this, unless he repented, he stood upon the considerations due to his birth and profession, and said he trusted that God would deal with him more like a gentleman!

Lieutenant Stern, the German, was a weak, superstitious man, in want of a penny, who, with the pliability to crime which is encouraged in such persons by certain notions of regeneration, had persuaded himself that he had nothing to do in the affair but stand by his friend Vratz, whom he understood to have intended only to fight a duel.

And lastly, poor stupid Borosky, the Pole whom the Lieutenant had seen intrusted with the loaded blunderbuss, and who, though the actual murderer, really seems to have been the least guilty of the three, had been brought up in the most senseless notions of the duty of a servant, and thought his sole business consisted in doing as his master told him.

We will present our readers, after this tragedy, with the dramatic refreshment of a bit of farce, in the person of a strange lumbering upstart of quality, who once figured in this polite region.

In Pall Mall, towards the close of the reign of George the Second, in the days of great lumbering coaches, bag-wigs, and burly suits of clothes, might be seen, coming up towards St James's, in a coach still more lumbering and a periwig to match, a huge corpulent figure of a man with his chin in the air and his eyelids hanging down, thinking of nothing but lords and levees. This was Bubb Doddington, Lord Melcombe Regis, author of the famous *Diary*, and the most creeping of all courtiers without knowing it. He even took a pride in his creeping. He gave himself the greatest airs, the more he was allowed to lick the way before him. Bubb, whose very name seemed to announce a bubble, was the son of an apothecary of that patronymic, and inherited the estate of a greater kinsman of the name of Doddington, on the strength of which he aspired to become a placeman and a lord, and did so.* He sold himself for a place to one party, for another to another, and for a title to a third. This *Diary*, which is an account of his rattings for such purposes, and of all the other servile measures he took to compass them, is written with such an extremity of shamelessness as amounts to simplicity, and has become an astonishment.

He never seems to dream that he is one of the meanest of mankind; nay, he lifts up his hands and eyes at people who act precisely as he does himself, "and all (as he says), for quarter day!"

Bubb had a mad self-ignorance, and was like a great gluttonous boy who sticks at nothing to compass his ends upon a pudding. Yet what renders the singularity of his case still more astonishing is, that this selfish overgrown simpleton included in his grosser nature a subordinate one, which was that of a witty, good-natured, and even liberal man; nay, a thinker and a man of taste. He wrote very pretty *vers de société;* was a sprightly and even argumentative speaker in Parliament; and patronised the cleverest men of the day, though his political profligacy at last made them ashamed of their very gratitude. Such, at least, was the case with good-natured Thomson, a man who would have allowed Bubb all his follies of the table, and his fine clothes, and perhaps even have admired his "swelling style," but who could not swallow a god in the shape of a turncoat.

Cumberland has given a most amusing account of Doddington in his Memoirs. When he went to and fro between Pall Mall and Hammersmith, where he had a house on the river-side, he was always driven in a coach drawn by "six fat unwieldy black horses;" his clothes were plastered with brocade and embroidery; and whether in town or country, he was to be approached only through a suite of apartments full of statues and pillars, was found sitting under painted ceilings and gilt entablatures, and slept in a bed over-canopied with peacock's feathers. In default of having a taste for pictures, he stuck bugle-horns about his principal room, cut out of gilt leather and fastened on hangings of crimson velvet; and round his state-bed was a carpeting of gold and silver embroidery, which, not to trench too deeply on "quarter-day," betrayed the secret of its origin by sundry loops, pockets, and button-holes; being, in fact, made out of his cast-off clothes. In short, Bubb was an amazing compound of wit, moralist, corruptionist, glutton, undertaker, orator, old-clothesman, grandee, reptile, and jolly fellow. Half a dozen ancestors must have crowded themselves into his single person; and a pretty business the Bubbs made of it with the Doddingtons. He represented them all at once, from the lord of the manor down to the most bowing of his menials, and from the fat lady in her ostrich feathers, to the cabbaging tailor and the jesting sexton.

CHAPTER XI.

SYDENHAM THE PHYSICIAN.—TOWN-HOUSES OF THE DUKES OF RUTLAND AND BUCKINGHAM.—EXTRAORDINARY ADVENTURE IN THE LATTER.— SOCIETY OF PAINTERS IN WATER-COLOURS.—COLLEGE OF PHYSICIANS.—COLNAGHI, STRONGI'TH'ARM, MOLTENO, ETC.,—MR MONCKTON MILNES. —SMOLLETT.—WEDDING CAKES.—EOTHEN AND WARBURTON.—STAR AND GARTER.—DUEL OF LORD BYRON AND MR CHAWORTH.

AMONG the inhabitants of Pall Mall, in the reign of Charles the Second, was the great physician Sydenham, who has been regarded as the father of modern medicine. He doubted the incurability of consumption, for which he recommended exercise on horseback; it is said with success. It has been wondered why he recommended the perusal of Don Quixote to Blackmore, when the latter applied to him respecting a course of medical reading. Probably Blackmore, who was a pedant, began by saying some foolish things in behalf of theory as superior to practice, which was the reverse of Sydenham's opinion. Perhaps the future bad poet was merely formal and dull; or, on the other hand, Sydenham may have meant to compliment him on his taste for the study of human nature, and advised him to cultivate it as the best help to the knowledge of his patients. Did he take Blackmore himself for a dull sort of Quixote? The new physician at all events did not like the advice. He used to tell the story with a foolish wonder, and was in the habit of undervaluing Sydenham; neither of which modes of recalling the circumstance to memory was calculated to remove its comic impression.

No. 85 was the town-house of the Rutland family,—a gallant and hospitable race, whose Conservatism does not hinder it from being beloved. A couplet from the pen of one of its junior members was accordingly received by the public some years ago with a good-natured smile. We believe it ran thus:

> "Let arts and commerce, laws and learning, die,
> But give us still our old nobility."

Alas! our old nobility, even in the pleasant shape of the Rutlands, would not last long, if deprived of the learning which gives it advantages of education, and the law which secures its property:—to say nothing of the luxuries which commerce brings it, and the arts which are the making of the Lord John Mannerses and the Lady Emmeline Stuart Wortleys. May all such good and graceful ascendancies prosper, till art, saving us meantime from the arrogancies both of aristocrat and democrat, gradually merges nobility itself into the nobility of the whole human race.

The title of Rutland is derived to the family of Manners from the Plantagenet house of York, in the annals of which it has been embalmed by one of the most pathetic, though least known, passages of Shakspeare. The familiar adjuration in the following lines is such as none but a master could venture on; but when so ventured, is of the deepest effect. We are to suppose it uttered by a manly voice, broken with tears. York is lamenting the death of his son Rutland, who, though a child, has been cruelly slain by the enemies of his house.

> These tears are my sweet Rutland's obsequies,
> And every drop cries vengeance for his death
> 'Gainst thee, fell Clifford, and thee, false Frenchwoman.

(He is speaking to Queen Margaret.)

> *Northumberland.* Beshrew me, but his passions move me so,
> That hardly can I check my eyes from tears.

> *York.* That face of his the hungry cannibals
> Would not have touch'd, would not have stain'd with blood:
> But you are more inhuman, more inexorable,—
> O, ten times more,—than tigers of Hyrcania.
> See, ruthless queen, a hapless father's tears:
> This cloth thou dipp'dst in blood of my sweet boy,
> And I with tears do wash the blood away.
> Keep thou the napkin, and go boast of this:
>
> *He gives back the handkerchief.*
>
> And if thou tell'st the heavy story right,
> Upon my soul, the hearers will shed tears;
> Yes, even my foes will shed fast-falling tears;
> And say,—Alas, it was a piteous deed!
>
> *Third part of King Henry the Sixth.*

Another ducal family, Buckingham (who are Grenvilles, and were ennobled by intermarriage with the Temples), had their town-house at No. 91. It was crowned by their coat of arms, and with what is called in heraldry a "canting motto;" that is to say, a motto punning on the family name,—"Templa quam dilecta" (how beloved are the Temples). The allusion is to a text in Scripture, "Lord, how beloved are thy temples." The family application is not so clear, and the effect cannot be called bashful. The Grenvilles have been an influential but not a popular generation. The Temples have been a livelier race, and produced more remarkable men, particularly in the branch of which Sir William Temple is the most famous ornament, and the present Lord Palmerston the eloquent representative. The motto of this portion of the family is of a different sort, "Flecti, non frangi" (You may bend, but not break). Mottoes are pretty things when they are good. It is a pity everybody does not adopt one. They are a kind of second conscience, at least to the adopter; or, at any rate, they serve as mementoes of reflection or inspiration. When hereditary, and not applicable, they often become rebukes of the most ludicrous description; as absurd as if a vulgar fellow were to mount on his hat a panegyric on politeness, or a sot a hymn to sobriety.

In this aristocratic abode once took place an act of so low a description as to be beneath vulgarity; for vulgarity implies commonness; and in what region but the lowest of the low could such a violation of feeling and common decency have been expected? The story is told by Horace Walpole. The parties were Lord Cobham (afterwards Earl Temple) and Lord Hervey, son of Pope's effeminate-looking Lord Hervey, and heir, it seems, to his father's delicacy of appearance.

"About ten days ago," says Walpole, "at the new Lady Cobham's assembly, Lord Hervey was leaning over a chair talking to some women, and holding his hat in his hand. Lord Cobham came up and spit in it—yes, spit in it!—and then, with a loud laugh, turned to Nugent, and said, 'Pay me my wager.' In short, he had laid a guinea that he committed this absurd brutality, and that it was not resented. Lord Hervey, with great temper and sensibility, asked if he had any further occasion for his hat?—' Oh! I see you are angry!' 'Not very well pleased.' Lord Cobham took the fatal hat and wiped it, made a thousand foolish apologies, and wanted to pass it for a joke. Next day he rose with the sun, and went to visit Lord Hervey; so did Nugent. He would not see them, but wrote to the spitter to say, that he had affronted him very grossly before company, but having involved Nugent in it, he desired to know to which he was to address himself for satisfaction. Lord Cobham wrote a most submissive answer, and begged pardon both in his own and Nugent's name. Here it rested for a few days, till, getting wind, Lord Hervey wrote again to insist on an explicit apology under Lord Cobham's own hand, with a rehearsal of the excuses that had been made to him. This, too, was complied with, and the *fair conqueror* shows all the letters."

Such can be the meeting of extremes, even

in places of refinement, when the refinement has become only an hereditary assumption, and the secret vulgarity seems to have been born on purpose to spite it. Who would have imagined this Earl Temple to be the successor of the Temple to whom Congreve addressed a poem on the *Art of Pleasing*, for his perfection in that delightful accomplishment? Suppose this gentleman could have foreseen a vision of his kinsman spitting into a hat! He would certainly have laid it all upon the Grenvilles, for the spitter was of that graft. But we think we see the solemn and weighty shade of the late Lord Grenville rising from the very dead to protest against the imputation.

The Club-houses in Pall Mall we pass over, intending to notice them all at once in our next chapter. Continuing, therefore, on the same side of the way into Pall Mall East, we observe the Society of Painters in Water-Colours (a truly English institution, excelling in wet and landscape), the College of Physicians (who scarcely seem to have warmed well into their new situation, after their renowned abode in the city), and the interesting print-shop of Messrs Colnaghi, in whose window you are pretty sure to see some fine things from the old masters, to say nothing of German imitations of them by new.

Returning into Pall Mall on the right hand, and again going through the arcade (opposite the end of which, by the way, the assassins of Thynne were *hung*), we pass the shop once occupied by the great seal-engraver with his terrible tranchant name, " Strongi'th'arm ; " then the Royal Society for the Prevention of Cruelty to Animals (causing odd misgiving glances to anglers); the house numbered 26, where in Parliament time lodged the right good philosophical poet and liberal Conservative, Richard Monckton Milnes; number 43, where at the like season, from the classical shire of

Dumbarton, of which he is still the representative, used to come a Smollett, descendant of the family renowned for that master of style and fun; number 44, the Star and Garter Tavern, of which more anon; number 51, once the shop of Mr Snowball Walker, "Wedding-cake Maker," sole artist (as far as we are aware) who confined himself to that denomination. He generally exhibited one sole cake in his window, knowing well enough what sweet worlds of association crowded around it. His otherwise contradictory Christian name, Snowball, typified of course nothing but the sugar on the top of the cake, and the white innocence of the purchasers. Number 52 is the British Institution, delightful for exhibitions of the old masters. We could never pass the window of No. 59, formerly Mr Ollivier's, the bookseller, without paying our respects to a volume in it— *Eothen*—in which men of reflection will find soundings of some of their deepest thoughts.

The author of this book, and his congenial friend Mr Warburton, are the two most suggestive and accomplished writers of travels which the lovers of that kind of reading have met with in England during the present century.

To return to the Star and Garter. In this tavern, in the year 1765, a duel took place which has acquired a fresh interest in the present day from the relationship of one of the parties to a late noble poet. A set of gentlemen were dining here, when a dispute arose on the subject of game between Lord Byron (great uncle of the poet) and his country neighbour, Mr Chaworth. Lord Byron was of opinion that the best way to preserve game was to take no care of it. Mr Chaworth was for being severe against poachers; adding, that there was not a hare in their part of the county of Nottingham which was not preserved either by him or Sir Charles Sedley. Lord Byron offered a bet of £100 that he had more game on a certain quantity of ground belonging to him than Sir Charles had on any such portion of his own. Chaworth accepted the wager; upon which his Lordship observed, in a tone of heat and sarcasm, "Sir Charles Sedley's manors! Where are his manors?" Chaworth, with equal warmth, replied, "The manors of Hucknell and Nuttall;" to which Lord Byron rejoined, "I know of no manors of Sir Charles Sedley." Chaworth said that one of them had been purchased from himself, and that if his Lordship wanted further information on the subject, Sir Charles was to be found in Dean-street, and he (Chaworth) in Berkeley Square.

The dispute here dropped, but on the party's breaking up, Lord Byron said he wished to speak to Mr Chaworth. They retired into a room by themselves, and here a duel with their swords immediately took place, of which they afterwards gave different accounts, and which ended in Chaworth's death. Chaworth intimated that there had been foul play. He would not distinctly assert it; but he remained silent when asked if it had been fair. He said that when he received the fatal thrust, the other's sword had been shortened to give it, and that his Lordship observed at the same time that "he hoped he would acknowledge he had as much courage as any other in the kingdom." Lord Byron averred, on the other hand, that everything had been done fairly. He was found guilty of manslaughter, and discharged on paying his fees.

It is impossible, of course, to say whether the duel was a fair one or not. Its intention might have been the foulest on both sides, seeing that it was fought without witnesses; and the survivor, whether guilty or unfortunate, could not but expect the odium which pursued him for the remainder of his life. He is said to have passed the latter years of it in a state of "austere and almost savage seclusion." The probability is, that he was a weak but not ill-natured man, conscious of a good deal of nervous sensibility, afraid of its being taken for cowardice, and hurried by his confusion into an irregularity of proceeding, the fatal consequences of which he bitterly repented.

This was one of the last duels that were fought with swords. The custom of investing the human animal with a sting, in the shape of a deadly weapon, by way of adding to the rashness and folly of which he had already quite enough, was beginning to go out of fashion; and it is not improbable that this equivocal adventure hastened its extinction.

CHAPTER XII.

CLUBS AND CO-OPERATION.—RISE AND VARIETY OF CLUBS.—EXTERIOR OF THOSE IN PALL MALL AND WATERLOO PLACE.—UNORIGINAL SPIRIT OF ENGLISH ARCHITECTURE.—BEAUTIES OF THE REFORM CLUB.—RECOLLECTION OF LAMAN BLANCHARD.—SUPERIORITY OF THE SPOT HEREABOUTS TO OTHER LONDON LOCALITIES.—YORK COLUMN, AND DEFENCE OF THE SOLITARY USE OF SUCH STRUCTURES.—NEIGHBOURS OF DIFFERENT RANK AND STATIONS.—PRINCE LOUIS BONAPARTE.—AMERICAN BOOKSELLERS.—RECORD OFFICE.—STATUE OF GEORGE THE THIRD.

So much has the co-operative principle been gaining ground in quarters which fancied themselves its most independent antagonists, that within these few years half the private houses on the south side of Pall Mall have been converted into what may be called magnificent public-houses, in which men club together to obtain good cookery. The poor of Mr Owen club in order that they may dine somehow; the rich and would-be rich of the West End (and a very natural "would-be" it is) do the same in order they may dine with Ude and Soyer. In these places people can pass the day as well as eat and drink; in some of them can sleep; in all can dress, amuse themselves, concert political and other measures; in short, enjoy the advantages both of home and of places of business without the ties of either. To judge by the Directories, many gentlemen and even noblemen live in them. There they give their addresses: and there, every day if they please, they can dine their friends, or dine *with* their friends on a picnic principle, without fear of inconveniencing my Lady, or suffering in the kitchen. The gentleman need not even make the old domestic apology—

"Supper and friends expect me at the Rose."

He is often expected nowhere else. The lady sits husbandless at home, and wonders whether Female Clubs will ever come up. She should ask her husband what he thinks of the "Whittington."

Not that we apprehend any great injury to the domesticities from these institutions. Those who are comfortable at home will like their own houses the better for the variety; and those who are not, had better, for the sake of all parties, be elsewhere. Still, the Whittington made a pretty compromise with the doubt; and set in motion a new principle of advancement.

We take clubs to be as old as companionship. There are signs of them in old eastern stories. Epicurus's sect was a sort of club; and so were the *Contubernales*, or tavern-companions, of Rome. The Freemasons boast to have been a universal club, time out of mind. Jachin and

Boaz are the symbolic pillars of their state. But the oldest clubs we hear of in England are no earlier than those of the Mermaid and the Devil Tavern — the clubs of Shakspeare and Ben Jonson. Then came the political clubs of the Commonwealth; then the whimsical excuses for bringing men together under the title of Odd Fellows, Ugly Fellows, Tall and Short Clubs, &c., as noticed in the *Spectator;* then the clubs of the wits under Dryden and others; of the *Spectator* himself (in the persons of Steele and Addison); and so on, through the gaming-clubs which Steele attacked, to their more refined brethren of White's and Brookes's, and the Literary Club of Dr Johnson. Clubs of a similar nature to all these exist at this moment; and, indeed, a considerable portion of the whole evening life of London may be said to be a club-life. Perhaps there are almost as many clubs as public-houses.

The principle, however, is quite a new one, by which men make up a common purse in order to secure uncommon and costly advantages. "Beefsteak Clubs" have met to enjoy a beef-steak, and the steak was to be well done; but there was no understanding that it was to be done cheaply; or at least, not with the advantages of the best cookery that money could obtain, and with the command of similar advantages on greater occasions and in twenty other respects. The principle is strictly co-operative in the modern sense of the word. The gentleman's every-day beef-steak is to be as well-cooked as the best lord's in the land; and he is to pay but little more for it than he paid at other places for a bad one. The cook himself is a gentleman; nay, an artist and a man of science, who understands things in their compounds, and laughs at the ignorance with which money and nourishment are thrown away.

The exteriors of these new club-houses have been much vaunted; but if the arrangements in the inside were not far better, the boast, generally speaking, would have little foundation. We are too apt in this country to suppose everything good which is new, big, and has cost money. As interiors, the clubs are admirable, particularly the Reform Club; but as exteriors there are but two that are worth stopping to look at—those of the club just mentioned and the Oxford and Cambridge. The frieze, it is true, on the Athenæum deserves attention, inasmuch as it is a copy from the Greek; and for the same reason it suits the name of the house; but then it painfully reminds us how difficult it is to get up any frieze of our own; and in other respects none of the houses, except the two above-mentioned, have an appearance beyond that of compactness and respectability. Indeed, they evidently aspire to nothing more, and should not be praised for what they never intended. To turn up the eyes in admiration at sight of a good honest deal box, or even at a piece of clever cabinet workmanship, and laud it as though it were a casket from the hand of Cellini, would be doing injustice to the box, and no honour to the man of genius.

The front of the Oxford and Cambridge Club is both substantial and ornamental. It has a solid elegance. How far it is original we cannot say; for the majority of English architects are either wholesale copyists, or commonplace bricklayers, or fantastic builders; and we pretend to no knowledge on the subject beyond that of some principles which are common to all the arts, and which anybody may learn by a little inquiry. Perhaps the builder deserves every credit for what we see; perhaps little or none except that of taste and adaptation. Even the Reform Club, which to an inexperienced eye has the most original as well as the most imposing aspect of all the club-houses, new or old, suggests to the travelled one the copy of an Italian mansion, and is, we believe, really such. It is understood to be imitated from one of the structures of Michael Angelo. At all events, it is an imitation in good taste, and on no sorry scale. It is simple, elegant, noble; and by the dignity of its presence absolutely crushes the poor Carlton and Traveller Clubs on each side of it, though one of these was built by the same artist. It also has the merit of being discernible, back and front, and thus of every way vindicating its pretensions. Perhaps the principal entrance might have been the better for a little more ornament or importance; but the whole composition is "simply great," and as striking as something ideal in a book. The spectator has only to fancy a southern sky over it, and some oleanders or myrtles at the sides, and he is in Italy. Then the little side entrance is, in our mind, perfectly elegant and beautiful; a thing to look at by itself, for its finish and proportions. It is like a cabinet of exquisite workmanship by the side of some chest of treasure.

We remember (if the reader will indulge us

a moment in the melancholy pleasure of the recollection) stopping to look at, and admire it, with poor dear Laman Blanchard, one fine summer night not long before he was taken ill, and when his mind was in its gentlest accustomed mood of a willingness to be pleased. As little should we have expected the sweet bit of architecture then before us to tumble suddenly into ruin and confusion, as to have looked for the end he came to. We ought not call him "poor," for with all his struggles he led for the most part a happy life, loving and beloved, and gave pleasure wherever he showed his face; nor can we ever think of the departure of a good spirit from this world but it seems enriched by its very passage into the grandeurs of the other. But it is the sorry living clay that must needs indulge its weakness in poor epithets. Truly we are "fearfully and wonderfully made," and liable to more fearful and wonderful changes. What a sudden, what a strange outrage and crash to a sweet lute was his! But discord is an ingredient in music itself; and the spirit of good and beauty will harmonize all.

Begging the reader's pardon for this bit of reverie by the way-side, we resume our journey.

We have already noticed Carlton House, which stood on the site of the present Carlton Gardens, of the York Column, and of the southern side of Waterloo Place. The spot, upon the whole, presents perhaps the handsomest collection of houses in the metropolis. Club, private house, and garden, conspire to set off one another; the back fronts, looking on the park with their lofty balconies, form the handsomest line of façade ever achieved by Mr Nash; and in spite of what is said about the anomaly of solitary pillars, we cannot help thinking that the York Column worthily crowns all. Not because the Duke of York worthily crowns the column; for though he was a gallant and well-natured prince, and we believe did more good to the soldiery by his general conduct in office than harm to any one by particular "slips," he was not a man, in any respect, of mark enough to warrant the elevation; but because an open space like this, so far from rendering a column unwarrantable, seems, in our opinion, to call for one, as its finish and contrast. We are aware, that although the architectural world practically take no heed of it, an opinion has been suffered to grow up that columns have no business to exist except as part and parcel of other buildings. They are pronounced to be limbs torn from bodies; things that have nothing to do but to support roofs and pediments, and monsters when used as pedestals, or standing alone. We confess our astonishment at the prejudice. A column no more belongs of necessity to another building than a tree belongs to a grove, a man to a multitude, or a woman with a basket of flowers on her head to Covent Garden Market. If a statue, for the sake of some exalting sentiment, is to be mounted aloft, what better can do it than a column? What else, indeed, to any lofty and particular purpose, can do it so well? And if its shape is beautiful, what is to hinder its being admired for its own sake? The worst of the York Column is, that it is a copy. It is borrowed, as usual, from the South. We scarcely ever find anything good among us in the shape of architecture, but we are reminded of our want of genius in the fine arts.

This spot, of which the York Column forms the centre, and Waterloo Place and Carlton Terrace the circumference, presents a curious mixture of associations, old and new, of the aristocratical and the innovating. Among the names of the inhabitants are Pembrokes, Clanricardes, and De Cliffords, mixed with those of gaming-house keepers and pushing tradesmen.

Here resides Sir William Temple's kinsman, Lord Palmerston, who has been accused of wishing to set Europe by the ears; and here, on his expedition against Louis Philippe, went forth Prince Louis Napoleon Bonaparte, who would infallibly have been obliged to fight his neighbour Lord Palmerston, could he have persuaded the French nation to take his uncle's cocked-hat for the brains that wore it. Here, at No. 3, Waterloo-place, resides the old Church-and-State bookselling firm of Rivington; while at No. 6 was to be found the American one of Wiley and Putnam (ominous-sounding names), who were helped to grow rich by unpaid English literature, because their ancestors threw off both Church and State, and mother country. An English man of letters certainly passes the doors of American booksellers in London with very singular feelings. He knows they will snatch hold of his book the moment it is published, sell thousands of copies of it on the other side of the Atlantic without giving him the benefit of a stiver, and perhaps have the pleasure of seeing him go by their London windows in the rain, while they are flourishing in a big house over his head. We suppose it is all right, and proper, and consistent, and free-born, and independent, and respectable, and slave-holding, and lovely, and going-a-head. It is certainly going another man's head, though with a considerable quantity of their own face beneath it. Yet, after all, "how they can do it," as the man said when he saw the New Zealand young gentlemen eating their benefactor, is to us inconceivable.

In a corner of this district, between Carlton Gardens and Warwick-street, and in a remnant of the buildings that once constituted the riding-house of the Prince of Wales—hence entitled Carlton-Ride—a passenger would have little expected to find an offset of the Rolls Office, containing some of the most precious records of English history and property. It was called the Record Office. The care and neatness, nay elegance, in which its venerable documents were kept by their intelligent supervisors, formed a singular contrast with the homeliness of their lodging. You literally went up and down among them by ladders, as if in a veritable stable, passing along alleys of lofts, and looking down into a gulf beneath. It was intended, we believe, to give them accommodation in the new Houses of Parliament; but the design was changed for we know not what other;—we think for a new building in their old quarters in Chancery-lane. It is a pity to see such interesting memorials, the last proofs of the existence of hundreds of old houses and monasteries, and often coloured as if with a remnant of their painted windows, huddled hither and thither for want of a proper resting-place.

We have now done with this particular

quarter, with the exception of one object, upon which it would have gratified us to say nothing. But it stands in the public way, and insists on being noticed. We allude to the equestrian statue of George the Third by the late Mr Wyatt, which presents itself to the passenger in the crossing by Pall-Mall East, and holds its hat in its hand as if emulating the claims of the street-sweeper. Its evident intention is to represent a high-bred horse in a state of elegant and impatient subordination, and a calm regal superiority on the part of the rider, whom we are to suppose saluting his beloved subjects, or returning perhaps the salutation of a regiment. It is not pleasant to find fault with anything that argues cleverness, and industry, and a purpose; but the work is over-done, and it is not characteristic. George the Third, whatever may have been his craft in some respects, or his self-possession in others, was a man both of plain habits and vehement impulses. He does not present himself to the imagination as a rider in a state of composure on a dandified palfrey. He and his horse should alike have been sturdy and unaffected; and, of the two, the expression of restlessness should have been on the human side.

CHAPTER XIII.

A WORD ON ISOLATED COLUMNS.—FRENCH THEATRE.—SUFFOLK-STREET.—SWIFT AND MISS VANHOMRIGH.— A WORD ON A REMARK MADE BY LOUIS NAPOLEON.—A DIGRESSION ON AMERICAN PIRACY. — PUNCH AND THE AMERICAN BOOKSELLERS.—PROFOUND AND PATERNAL CHARACTER OF PUNCH.—HIS OPINION RESPECTING THE CONDUCT OF AMERICAN BOOKSELLERS TO ENGLISH AUTHORS.—REMARKS OF "THE TIMES" ON THE SAME SUBJECT.

ONE of the objections to putting statues at the top of columns is that they are not to be seen, that the features become indistinguishable. This is true; but the presence of the statue is felt; the honour done to the original is felt; the greater the elevation, the loftier and more overlooking becomes the glory; and this is the main object of a statue so placed. It is the elevation of a sentiment, the ascendancy of a name and a nature.

In our observations on noteworthy places, we have omitted to mention a prominent public building in the district of St James, to wit, the St James's Theatre. The theatre deserves praise for its elegant exterior and for the lively French plays and performers, which are an importation among us of animal spirits.

Suffolk Street ought to be mentioned if it were for nothing but its association, however painful, with the memory of Swift, who was a great original and a classic. It was here that he made love (or led her to think so) to poor Miss Vanhomrigh, a warm-hearted girl of eighteen, who became enamoured of the wit and fame of a man of forty-four. Swift (in whose days clergymen wore their canonicals out of doors) used to leave his " best gown " at her mother's house in this street when he lodged at Chelsea; and to call and put it on, and entertain the young lady when he came to town. Miss Vanhomrigh found out that the great wit was engaged to another woman, and she broke her heart. At least, she died not long afterwards. And the other lady, poor Stella (Miss Johnson), had but a strange, mysterious time of it in her intercourse with Swift. She was married to him, yet never saw him alone. The secret has never been explained. Whatever it was, vanity was probably at the bottom of it, in the first instance—the charm of conquering hearts which he had no business to appropriate. Such male coquetry (had it even been nothing else) would have been criminal enough in a youth, and sufficient to produce the pangs which the husband of Stella appears to have felt on her account in the decline of life; but to play with the happiness of people in their teens at the age of forty-four, would seem to argue the most determined selfishness, let the temptation to middle-aged vanity have been what it might.

Suffolk-street has been rebuilt, but it stands on the same ground, so that it has a right to the old associations; and as time, among its other good offices, bestows the same mellow and softening colour on circumstances as it does on pictures, we are sorry we cannot point out the exact spot, or the number of the house in which "Vanessa," as Swift called her, sat at the receipt of praises from wits and visits from people of quality. She was the daughter of a Dutch merchant, and inherited a fortune. The following passage from the Dean's poem of *Cadenus and Vanessa* presents some traits of manners in those times:—

> "A party next of glittering dames,
> From round the purlieus of St James,
> Come early out of pure good-will
> To see the girl in deshabille.
> Their clamour, 'lighting from their chairs,
> Grew louder all the way up-stairs;
> At entrance loudest, where they found
> The room with volumes littered round.

> Vanessa held Montaigne, and read,
> Whilst Mrs Susan combed her head.
> They called for tea and chocolate,
> And fell into their usual chat,
> Discoursing with important face
> On ribbons, furs, and gloves and lace;
> * * * * *
> Dear Madam, let me see your head;
> Don't you intend to put on red?
> A petticoat without a hoop!
> Sure, you are not ashamed to stoop."

Suffolk-street is as old, at least, as 1678; for in that year Stanley, the author of the *Lives of the Philosophers*, died there, and was buried in St Martin's Church. It next became famous for the Calves-head Club, a disgraceful jest on the fate of Charles the First. Adam Smith lodged in it during one of his sojourns in London; and it has been paced by everybody connected with the Haymarket Theatre, the back of which opens into it, and is a residence of the manager.

Before we proceed on our route we beg the reader's indulgence while we say a word or two on a passage which has appeared in a letter addressed to the newspapers, by Prince Louis Napoleon Bonaparte. This illustrious person, in repelling a charge made against him of violating his word with the King of the French, accuses public opinion of being inexorable towards the fallen. We do not assume that the prince had any knowledge of the few trifling words which we said of him on a previous occasion; much less that, if he had, they would have given him any concern; but having used them, and feeling ourselves blush at the bare imagination of being thought capable, by any one, of joining in the injustice he speaks of, we must not only express the feeling accordingly, but take the opportunity of saying that we think the writer of the letter mistaken, and that the world in general are far from being inexorable towards the fallen. Probably the idea of the Prince's being "fallen" enters into their heads as little as into ours; but in case it does, we suspect he has the full benefit of it, and that they spare him a proportionate amount of the objections which they may think he deserves for having needlessly attempted to disturb the peace of Europe; to say nothing of the style in which the attempt was made. We mention this as the feeling of the world at large, and not of course in any forward or absurd spirit of our own as an individual; a character, the imputation of which it perplexes us quite enough to keep clear of on smaller matters. Nobody but the members of a narrow-minded administration, who were jealous of his title of "Emperor," was severe upon the Prince's fallen uncle at St Helena; certainly not, at all events, till he condescended to quarrel with his gaoler. Nobody has been severe on the Prince's good father, Louis, King of Holland; nobody on his accomplished mother, Queen Hortense; nobody (that we are aware of) on any member of the Bonaparte family, unless it may have been some particular French faction quarrelling with another. The world may be severe on certain failures, or modes of failure; but with reverse of fortune, generally speaking, especially when connected with great qualities, it has a warm and honourable sympathy. It felt for Napoleon even though he had forsaken freedom; it felt for Murat; it respected Napoleon's countryman, Paoli; and it adored Kosciusko.

We have to make our acknowledgments to our formidable, facetious, but no less reflecting and paternal contemporary, *Punch;* who is pleased to approve these our pedestrian discourses in general, and what we said of the American booksellers in particular. We say, advisedly, "reflecting and paternal"—(a phase of character in which our contemporary's likeness has been so happily caught by his portrait-painter, Mr Leech)—for though, on the wrapper of his publication, our distinguished friend condescends to wear that carnival or masquerade aspect, under which in his old world-famous character he still enlightens his street-audiences on the stoical part of the philosophy of animal spirits, and gives and receives such prodigious quantities of knocks on the head, with a crow and a chuckle which their utmost calamitousness cannot subdue; yet, unquestionably, when he appears in those staider and more well-bred habiliments which generally adorn him in the interior of his pages, nobody can deny that he is the pink of elderly respectability, or hesitate to expect from him all those benefits to the world which are announced by the union of a smile a yard long with an eye that can retreat into a commensurate depth of meditation. The excess, it is true, of some advantages on the side of the rich and courtly may occasionally provoke our friend into an apparent extreme of antagonism, by way of giving a better adjustment to the balance; but a perspicacity so universal as his, recognises, of necessity, the circumstances of which rich and poor are equally the creatures; and hence there is no man who feels himself more finally at his ease than *Punch* does in the very highest society, owing to the dignified consciousness of his motives as well as the martial ascendancy of his aspect. He knows what is due, in the best corners of all quarters, to the suppressor of shams and the elevator of things real.

To drop eulogies, however, of which our illustrious friend has no need, we proceed to observe, that while he agrees with us on the necessity of admonishing the American booksellers, and would "persuade" and even "shame" them "into honesty," he speaks of the right principles having been recognised by Congress (a circumstance we were not aware of), and expresses a confident expectation that the booksellers themselves will eventually, "like *Mrs Chick*, make an effort to be decent, and cease to become the *Fagins* of letters, the very respectable dealers in stolen goods."

Since these and other strong remarks on the subject were made by *Punch*, the *Times* has noticed a striking instance of the unhandsome system in question. A living English writer of great beauty and eloquence, particularly charming for his graces of expression (the Rev. Robert Aris Willmott), is author of a Biography of Jeremy Taylor, which was lately reviewed in that journal. The review no sooner appears, than the good money-making news is sent across the Atlantic, and the following announcement is seen in the journals of America: "Messrs Wiley and Putnam will publish immediately, 'Jeremy Taylor, a Biography, by the Rev. R. A. Willmott.'"

Upon this the *Times* remarks:—

"We had occasion to speak lately in terms

of unqualified praise of a biography of Jeremy Taylor, by the Rev. R. Aris Willmott. A New York paper, the *Literary World*, the last number of which has just reached us, contains an elaborate review of Mr Willmott's work, in which we are pleased to recognise a full appreciation of its merits. Nothing can be more gratifying to the just vanity of an author than to find a new world added to the number of those who read and admire the fruit of his labours Authors, however, like other mortals, may justly expect a more solid reward than fame; and we confess it is with a feeling of mortification, if not of disgust, that we find in the same paper in which the review appears an announcement that Messrs Wiley and Putnam will publish immediately 'Jeremy Taylor, a Biography, by the Rev. R. A. Willmott.' With no copyright to pay for, a cheap reprint of Mr Willmott's work will circulate through every district of the States; and though he may rejoice that the high character and exemplary virtues of one of the best of England's bishops are thus made known to thousands who would otherwise have probably never heard his name, he must have all the sweetness of temper of his hero, if he can view with complacency the large profits which the American publishers are making at the expense of his labour and tasteful scholarship."

Yes; and we know not how the case is with Mr Willmott—men of his delicacy of feeling are seldom apt to be too rich—but Jeremy's sweet temper might well have been allowed a variation of bitterness, had he been struggling for his family in these days, as he was obliged at one time to do in his own, and then seen the booksellers of another country lying in wait to pocket his productions, perhaps, too, after his circumstances had forced him to make a bad bargain for them at home. As to the gratification experienced by an author at seeing his writings welcomed in the New World, it is very true; and the rogues know it. They tell him of it; boast of it; talk of the thousands they have circulated of his "delightful work;" congratulate him on it with an air of generous interest in his fame, the more provoking from the flagrant selfishness that actuates them; and perhaps conclude by informing him, that they hope to be the means of diffusing as many thousands of his "delightful *new* work," with which they have just heard he has "favoured the public." They know, not only that the author meantime is glad of the increase of his readers out of a feeling of vanity, but that he ought to be glad of it, on a higher principle, if he thinks his writings good for the world. They take therefore to themselves the merit of being aiders of virtue and diffusers of liberal opinion, and thus crown their engagingness by what the philosopher calls the most exasperating of all effronteries; namely, the doing an unjust thing on the pretence of its being just.

These " drab-coloured men," or copper-coloured men, the receivers of stolen goods, will certainly hear more of this from our English writers if they do not reform. The Sydney Smiths are many, in *Punch* and other papers; and even rogues do not like to be made ridiculous. Let them reflect in time. Booksellers are men, even in America; and unfortunately men can be led by some reigning vice to do things in one unjust respect which they would be ashamed to do in another. *Punch* is in hopes that the American booksellers will mend; and we should be sorry to say anything to provoke them into sulkiness and thus hinder the good change. We say this in order to show them that we are as much prepared to do justice to their better impulses, as to assist in shaming them out of the injustice of their present; and we will even venture to add (for every appearance of a concession is venturous with some persons, however unreal it may be, except in reference to some collateral accident, or at best to some human inconsistency) that we are sorry to call the subject to mind at a moment when their country has shown its participation in the sympathy with Ireland. We never said that the Americans were brutes, or wanted common feeling, even though they retained their slaves when they proclaimed themselves free, and have since been exasperated by fear and error into worse defences of that mistake. We are aware also of the many excellent men among them, who hold the best and handsomest opinions on all subjects. But it is really high time that those who claim the right of admiring such men, and of being received among their respectable fellow-citizens in the class of trade and commerce, should cease to aid in the deterioration of the national character by lowering the money-making part of it to its unhandsomest condition, and plundering the authors of other countries. It is not respectable; it is not decent; it is not even "shrewd," and "clever," and "going-a-head," if success is to be anything better than a paltry strongbox, with a loss of nine out of ten of the keys that can open it to any ultimate satisfaction.

For our part, we can safely say, that had we been rich, or possessed of a competence, or been able in any way to dispense with the profits of our productions (political circumstances having caused us to be at a disadvantage in that respect, which we have never recovered), the American booksellers would have been as heartily welcome to all the books we wrote, as we should have been pleased to write them. Our lot would be too blest, could we write what we pleased, send out our book or so in due season from pure love of the subject, and see anybody make a penny of it but ourselves. And we must add, that we are so little accustomed to complain, or to resent any profit which others can make of us, that in all probability we should never have said a word of the American booksellers, had not the subject presented itself to us accidentally.

CHAPTER XIV.

APOLOGY FOR LONG DIGRESSIONS.—A FEW WORDS MORE IN CONNECTION WITH THE DAYS OF THE PRINCE REGENT. — POLITICAL RECOLLECTIONS. — SUCCESS OF LIBERAL MEASURES. — INDICTMENT AGAINST THE AUTHOR. — A COSTLY JEST. — A FEW WORDS MORE ON THE DOINGS OF AMERICAN BOOKSELLERS.—BUCKINGHAM HOUSE.— SHEFFIELD AND HIS DUCHESS. — CHARACTER OF QUEEN CHARLOTTE.—HER MAJESTY'S FAVOUR FOR MISS BURNEY (MADAME D'ARBLAY).

THOUGH our subject tends as naturally to digression as main streets do to smaller ones, yet we are sorry to depart from it once more on a matter relating personally to ourselves. But circumstances having led us to speak of what we have undergone in behalf of the now reigning opinions in politics, and blushing (as we confess we did) to see how much we had said when our remarks came before us in print, yet in vindication of what we hope we may call our natural delicacy we have to observe—first, that we have ever been accustomed to "wear our heart on our sleeve;" secondly, that although the claims which we are thought to possess upon a considerate Administration have never before been publicly alluded to by ourselves, they have frequently been mooted in literary and political circles; thirdly, that a considerable and distinguished portion of the periodical press has advocated them, without distinction of parties (a circumstance of inexpressible comfort to us); and, lastly, that unless ill-health conspires with age to deceive us, time presses, and "the night cometh in which no man can work." At the same time, we beg the reader to understand, that we say all this in no whining or lamenting tone. Neither shall we complain of anybody, whatever happens; nor, after this, say a word more on the subject. Life, upon the whole, though a severely tried, has been a strenuous and cheerful thing with us; and we mean to do our best that it shall remain so to the last. We look upon ourselves as having personally succeeded in the tasks which we set it—namely, the doing some good to the world, and the gaining some portion of repute as a writer; and if we fear that we might have included a greater amount of benefit to young persons who are dear to us, perhaps, by and by, should they have need of its good will, the world will look not without tenderness on our memory.

Almost every liberal measure that has since become a deed of the State—perhaps we might say, every one without exception, from Catholic Emancipation to the Anti-Corn-Laws—did we advocate in the most trying times, when Toryism was at the height of its power, and when almost everybody, even its quondam friends, was trying to blow out the little taper of Reform, then kept alive by some half-dozen writers. We had even to defend it (it may not be the best thing for us to say, and yet it is good for generous men to hear) against our old friends the Edinburgh Reviewers. We shall not enlarge on that recollection; much less attempt to recall distinctions of party now dying away; but perhaps we should have reason to think it a little hard, if the generals of the old army, or their representatives, should still leave us lying on the field of battle, after we had done our best to keep the fight alive, and had fought inch by inch for what it seemed fit to their strategy to abandon. When the battle was finally over, honest men of all parties shook hands. They all had perhaps something to forgive one another. They did so as human beings, conscious of good motives and of liability to error; and it is one of our proudest and most consolatory reflections, that some of our warmest public friends at this instant were among those who fought us hardest in the *mêlée*. We think, to be sure, that while we were about it, they carried the license of war to an immoderate extent on the side of fancy and misrepresentation; and people who live in the present quiet times have no conception of the consequences even of a temporary defeat in those days. Men lost their properties and were driven from their homes by the fierce ascendancy of the conquerors; and the more a writer was in advance of the reigning opinions, the more the very "trade" avoided him, or subjected him to the most exacting and nullifying treatment. It is different now; and the most speculative writers may recover their fortunes, if they are young and healthy enough. But while opinions are changing, people grow old; and this it is, we apprehend, which gives an old soldier a right to look on his wounds, and think it would be no dishonour to those he has fought for to heal them. There is authorship among the present ministers; there is genius (which is the twin of geniality or sympathy); there is experience of trouble; there is family affection; there is even, in more than one quarter of it, personal good-will towards the individual in question; and if he wants the *prestige* of the "circles," this, he conceives, is not what a reasonable claim of any sort is bound to bring with it, or what the next generation (supposing it to consider the matter at all) would hold to have been an indispensable requisite, even on the side of refinement.

We have thus stated the general political grounds of the claims in question. Let us be allowed to recur for a moment to those particulars of them, from which the writer more immediately suffered.

Think of an action having been brought against him by Government for making use of the following words:—" Of all Monarchs since the Revolution, the successor of George the Third will have the finest opportunity of becoming nobly popular!"

This was said out of the innocence of his belief in the possible good faith and liberal intentions of the Prince of Wales; little suspecting that his Royal Highness would one day return the compliment by making him suffer for the simplicity.

Think of an indictment having been laid against him by the same Government for copying out of a provincial journal a paragraph against military flogging, not half so severe as what was lately uttered against it every day in half the papers of the kingdom. We do not remember the words, and have them not at hand to refer to. We were acquitted on that and on the former charge, but not without being considerably out of pocket from both; the law strangely considering it compatible with its dignity to burden a man with the expenses of government-prosecutions, even when it fails to establish the grounds of them.

But think, above all, of the writer's having been condemned to a fine of five hundred pounds and two years' imprisonment for contradicting the Tory adulations of the *quondam* Whig Prince, and saying that if he was an " Adonis " (as they actually called him), he was an " Adonis of fifty." For though this jest was accompanied by graver and severer words, it is well understood that the sting of the objection lay in the venerableness of the dandyism, and that if his Royal Highness's pretensions had been less founded on external appearance, he could have afforded to forgive the rest. Indeed, the rest would have been self-refuted. Our present sovereign, though a woman, and young, and innocent, and estimable, was once assailed by a strange remnant of Tories, now defunct, with some of the worst insinuations. But what was her answer? A serene silence. She turned, as it were, with a face of dignified confidence towards the mass of her subjects, and they almost disdained to think it necessary even to scorn the calumniators. We may as well take this occasion of adding, that our remarks on the Prince Regent were excited, not only by the most preposterous adulations of his new friends (absolute assertions of his being a pattern of loveliness in " shape and face "), but by the concurrent indignation of all his quondam friends for his having broken his promises to the Whigs in general and to the Irish Catholics in particular. The article in which the remarks appeared was on the subject of "St Patrick's Day," and the writer of it, though as little Popish in his doctrines then as he is now, but as much in favour of toleration to all sorts of conscientious opinions as he has been ever, was moved to express himself as warmly as he did by the refusal of that long-promised concession to the Catholic claims, which, had it been made as early as it should have been, would not only have saved the Prince Regent from some of the charges made against him by his old friends, but have prevented all that reaction of late years in favour of superstition, which, however transient and absurd, has been the cause of no little scandal to the kingdom.*

Having thus explained the writer's claims on

* The writer's brother, who partook of all these trials, ultimately suffered still further in the cause of Reform, both in purse and person, with invincible courage; but as he never ceased to retain a hold on the property of the *Examiner*, was subjected to no critical hostilities, and has not had the same anxious career to run for a family, the privacy of his affairs has, of course, not been trespassed upon in these recitals. The fine exacted of us in conjunction, in the case of the Prince Regent, was a thousand pounds. The other legal expenses on the three indictments, and the cost of the two years' imprisonment, brought our losses altogether much nearer to a second thousand than to the total intimated in the previous remarks on this subject. But the writer desires to be under the mark. One of the worst consequences to himself was the deterioration of a delicate state of health, from which he afterwards severely suffered, and which threw the greatest difficulties in the way of a retrieval of his finances.

a liberal Ministry as much further as his first notice of them seemed to render necessary, and taking the opportunity of again expressing his trust in that good will of theirs towards him, for the manifestation of which it was the chief object of the explanation to show that they would have just and sufficient warrant (supposing such evidence to be needed towards a new generation), we turn for another moment to the question respecting the American booksellers. It will be only for a moment; because the matter must take some larger and more distinct form of discussion, unless (as we hope is possible) they may choose to adopt some measures for proving those better impulses on the subject, to the credit of which they lay claim. Mr Putnam, the American bookseller, has written to the *Times*, asserting that the English booksellers are as bad as those of his own country; that they would not give authors more for their works, though America should cease to reprint them; that meantime *some* English authors do receive *something* from America; and that for his own part, he (with the American booksellers in general) would gladly see an international law on the subject, and has done his best to procure one. He asserts, at the same time, that he does not see why booksellers should not avail themselves of the absence of laws on the subject, till laws be made; though he acknowledges, as an abstract proposition, that two wrongs (the American and the English) do not make a right. Mr Bentley, in answer to this letter, has indignantly and triumphantly stated, as far as regards himself, that he pays large sums for American copyrights; and here the matter for the present has dropped. It is obvious that Mr Putnam is only playing with the subject, not with a very good conscience; and we shall confine ourselves for the present to a few brief remarks; first, that the English booksellers deny that they would give no more to their authors in case those of America ceased to reprint their books; second, that in case of that cessation it is obvious that any English work sold in America must somehow or other give the English authors a greater chance of remuneration; third, that there is a great craving for English works in America, which the English authors or booksellers would have in that case exclusively to supply, so that it would be the authors' own fault if their countrymen did not pay them accordingly; fourth, that in the mean time they are egregiously plundered, Mr Putnam himself evidently thinking so: and fifth, that Mr Putnam, who endeavours to salve his conscience on the point by the sorry plea of there being no law to hinder him, might with as much justice be deprived of the fruits of his own industry by any gentleman of the swell mob who could keep within the letter of the statutes.

Mr Putnam accuses the English authors of having delayed the settlement of the question by "abuse," and perhaps he will think the preceding remark abusive. We are not the men to deny to any human being the right of referring to custom and breeding for particular excuses, and we shall not deny it to Mr Putnam; but it is rather hard, and not a little cool, that verbal abuse (if there has been any) should be alleged as a reason why a gross practical abuse should be maintained. What would Mr Putnam say to a man, who, being detected in walking off with his plate, and not unnaturally being addressed in no very courteous words, should turn round and say, "Come—a little more civility, if you please—or you'll not have your spoons back in a hurry."

Resuming for a moment our street perambulations, we shall bring them to an end, at least for the present, by some remarks on Buckingham House, and on one or two of its former inmates. Not long after the marriage of George the Third, Buckingham House was settled on his young Queen, in the event of her surviving him; and the King took such a liking to it as to convert St James's Palace wholly into a resort for state occasions, and confine his town residence to the new abode. Buckingham House was so called from John Sheffield, Duke of Buckinghamshire, who built it. It was a dull though ornamented brick edifice, not unworthily representing the mediocre ability and stately assumptions of the owner, who was a small poet and a fastidious grandee, nearly as mad with pride as his duchess. This lady was a natural daughter of James the Second (if indeed she was even that, for a Colonel Godfrey laid claim to the paternity), and she carried herself so loftily in consequence, as to wish to be treated seriously as a princess, receiving visitors under a canopy and going to the theatre in ermine. She and the Duchess of Marlborough, who had a rival palace, next door to St James's, used to sit swelling at one another with neighbourly spite. Sheffield, her husband, is said to have first made love to her sister Anne (afterwards Queen), for which her uncle, Charles the Second, has been accused of sending him on an expedition to Tangier in a "leaky vessel."

The Duke wrote a long, complacent description of Buckingham House, that has often been reprinted, recording, among other things, the classical inscriptions which he put upon it, and the princely chambers which it contained for the convenience of the births of his illustrious house. The births came to nothing in consequence of the death of his only legitimate child; a natural son inherited the property, and Government bought it for Queen Charlotte. Henceforward it divided its old appellation of Buckingham House with that of the "Queen's House;" almost all the Queen's children were born there; and there, as at Kew and Windsor, she may be said to have secreted her husband as much as she could from the world, partly out of judicious consideration for his infirmities, and partly in accordance with the pride as well as penuriousness that were at the bottom of manners not ungentle, and a shrewd though narrow understanding.

The spirit of this kind of life was very soon announced to the fashionable world after her marriage by the non-appearance of certain festivities; and it continued as long as her husband lived, and as far as her own expenditure was concerned; though when her son came to the throne she astonished the public by showing her willingness to partake of festivities in an establishment not her own. A deplorable exhibition of her tyrannous and unfeeling habits of exaction from the attentions of those about her was alluded to in our reference to the *Diary of Madame d' Arblay* (Miss Burney), whom they almost killed with consumption. It is clear that they would have done so, had not the poor waiting-gentlewoman mustered up courage enough to dare to save her life by persisting in her request to be set free.

Queen Charlotte was a plain, penurious, soft-spoken, decorous, bigoted, shrewd, overweening personage, " content " through a long life " to dwell in decencies for ever," inexorable " upon principle " to frailty, but not incapable of being bribed out of it by German prepossessions and whatever else might assist to effect the miracle; as was seen in the instance of Mrs Hastings, who had been Warren Hastings's mistress, and who was, nevertheless, received at court. Pleasant as her Majesty might have been to Miss Burney, who seems to have loved to be "persecuted," she was assuredly no charmer in the eyes of the British nation; nor was she in the slightest degree lamented when she died. Nevertheless she was a very good wife, for such we really believe her to have been; we mean not merely faithful (for who would have tempted her?), but truly considerate, and anxious, and kind; and besides this she had another merit, not indeed of the same voluntary description, but one for which the nation is strongly indebted to her, though we are not aware that it has ever been mentioned. We mean that her cool and calculating brain turned out to be a most happy match for the warmer one of her husband, in ultimate as well as immediate respects; for it brought reason back into the blood of his race, and drew a remarkable line in consequence between him and his children; none of whom, however deficient in abilities, partook of their father's unreasonableness, while some went remarkably counter to his want of orderliness and self-government.

The happy engraftment of the Coburg family on the stock completed this security in its most important quarter; and if ever a shade of more than ordinary sorrow for the necessity should have been brought across the memory in that quarter by a ridiculous pen, the sense of the security ought to fling it to the winds, with all the joy and comfort befitting the noblest brow, and the wisest reign, that have yet adorned the annals of its house.

THE END.

JOHN CHILDS AND SON, PRINTERS.

13, Great Marlborough Street.
MESSRS HURST AND BLACKETT'S
NEW PUBLICATIONS.

HENRY IV., AND MARIE DE MEDICI; FORM-
ING PART II. OF THE HISTORY OF THE REIGN OF HENRY IV., KING OF FRANCE AND NAVARRE. From Original and Authentic Sources. By Miss Freer, Author of "The Lives of Marguerite D'Angoulême, Jeanne D'Albret, Elizabeth de Valois, Henry III., &c. 2 vols.,with Portraits, 21s.

THE OKAVANGO RIVER; A NARRATIVE OF
TRAVEL, EXPLORATION, AND ADVENTURE. By Charles John Andersson. Author of "Lake Ngami." 1 vol., with Portrait and numerous Illustrations. (Just ready.)

MEMOIRS OF THE COURTS AND CABINETS OF
WILLIAM IV. AND VICTORIA. From Original Family Documents. By the Duke of Buckingham, K.G. 2 vols., 8vo, with Portraits.

ESSAYS FROM THE QUARTERLY. By James Hannay. 8vo.

TRAVELS IN THE REGIONS OF THE AMOOR,
AND THE Russian Acquisitions on the Confines of India and China; By T. W. Atkinson, F.G.S., F.R.G.S., Author of "Oriental and Western Siberia." Dedicated, by permission, to Her Majesty. Second Edition, Royal 8vo, with Map and 83 Illustrations. £2 2s. elegantly bound.

RECOLLECTIONS OF A FOX HUNTER. By "Scrutator." 1 vol., with Illustrations.

THE ENGLISH SPORTSMAN IN THE WEST-
ERN PRAIRIES. By the Hon. Grantley Berkeley. 1 vol., Royal 8vo, with numerous Illustrations.

SEASONS WITH THE SEA HORSES; or Sport-
ing Adventures in the Northern Seas. By James Lamont, F.G.S. 1 vol., 8vo, with numerous Illustrations.

THE MEDICAL MISSIONARY IN CHINA: A
Narrative of Twenty Years' Experience. By William Lockhart, F.R.C.S., of the London Missionary Society. Second Edition. 1 vol., 8vo.

JAVA; OR, HOW TO MANAGE A COLONY. By J. W. B. Money, Esq. 2 vols., 21s.

TEN YEARS' WANDERINGS AMONG THE
ETHIOPIANS. By T. J. Hutchinson, F.R.G.S., Consul for Fernando Po. 1 vol., 14s.

A BOOK ABOUT DOCTORS. By J. C. Jeaffreson, Esq. Second and Cheaper Edition, Revised. 1 vol., 10s. 6d.

MEMOIRS OF ROYAL LADIES. By Emily S. Holt. 2 vols., with Portraits.

UNDER THE ESPECIAL PATRONAGE OF HER MAJESTY
AND H. R. H. THE PRINCE CONSORT.

Published annually in December, in one Volume, royal 8vo, with the Arms beautifully Engraved, Handsomely Bound, with Gilt Edges, Price 31s. 6d.,

LODGE'S PEERAGE
AND BARONETAGE.
ARRANGED AND PRINTED FROM THE PERSONAL COMMUNICATIONS OF THE
NOBILITY, AND CORRECTED THROUGHOUT TO THE TIME OF PUBLICATION.

LODGE'S PEERAGE AND BARONETAGE is acknowledged to be the most complete, as well as the most elegant, work of the kind. As an established and authentic authority on all questions respecting the family histories, honours, and connections of the titled aristocracy, no work has ever stood so high. It is published under the especial patronage of Her Majesty and His Royal Highness the Prince Consort, and is annually corrected throughout, from the personal communications of the Nobility. It is the only work of its class in which, *the type being kept constantly standing*, every correction is made in its proper place to the date of publication, an advantage which gives it supremacy over all its competitors. Independently of its full and authentic information respecting the existing Peers and Baronets of the realm, the most sedulous attention is given in its pages to the collateral branches of the various noble families, and the names of many thousand individuals are introduced, which do not appear in other records of the titled classes. Nothing can exceed the facility of its arrangements, or the beauty of its typography and binding, and for its authority, correctness, and embellishments, the work is justly entitled to the high place it occupies on the tables of Her Majesty and the Nobility.

" Lodge's Peerage must supersede all other works of the kind, for two reasons; first, it is on a better plan; and, secondly, it is better executed. We can safely pronounce it to be the readiest, the most useful, and exactest of modern works on the subject."
—*Spectator*.

"A work which corrects all errors of former works. It is the production of a herald, we had almost said, by birth, but certainly by profession and studies, Mr Lodge, the Norroy King at Arms. It is a most useful publication."—*Times*.

" As perfect a Peerage of the British Empire as we are ever likely to see published. Great pains have been taken to make it as complete and accurate as possible. The work is patronised by Her Majesty and the Prince Consort; and it is worthy of a place in every gentleman's library, as well as in every public institution."—*Herald*.

" As a work of contemporaneous history, this volume is of great value—the materials having been derived from the most authentic sources, and in the majority of cases emanating from the noble families themselves. It contains all the needful information respecting the nobility of the Empire."—*Post*.

"When any book has run through twenty-eight editions, its reputation is so indelibly stamped, that it requires neither criticism nor praise. It is but just, however, to say, that 'Lodge's Peerage and Baronetage' is the most elegant and accurate, and the best of its class."—*Messenger*.

" This work should form a portion of every gentleman's library. At all times, the information which it contains, derived from official sources exclusively at the command of the author, is of importance to most classes of the community; to the antiquary it must be invaluable, for implicit reliance may be placed on its contents."—*Globe*.

HURST AND BLACKETT, PUBLISHERS, 13, GREAT MARLBOROUGH STREET.

NOW IN COURSE OF PUBLICATION,

HURST AND BLACKETT'S STANDARD LIBRARY
OF CHEAP EDITIONS OF
POPULAR MODERN WORKS.

Each in a single volume, elegantly printed, bound, and illustrated, price 5s. A volume to appear every two months. The following are now ready.

VOL. I.—SAM SLICK'S NATURE AND HUMAN NATURE
ILLUSTRATED BY LEECH

Messrs Hurst and Blackett have very fitly inaugurated their Standard Library of Popular Modern Works with this admirable volume. With regard to this we can truly say:—Who can tire of the genuine sallies, the deep wisdom wrapped up in merry guise, and the side-splitting outbursts of genuine wit, in the pages of Haliburton? 'Nature and Human Nature' is particularly full of all these qualities; and to those who love a good laugh, when they can enjoy it accompanied by good matter for reflection, and who have not yet read this production of Sam Slick, we can heartily recommend this elegant Edition."—*Critic.*

"The first volume of Messrs Hurst and Blackett's Standard Library of Cheap Editions forms a very good beginning to what will doubtless be a very successful undertaking. 'Nature and Human Nature' is one of the best of Sam Slick's witty and humorous productions, and well entitled to the large circulation which it cannot fail to obtain in its present convenient and cheap shape. The volume combines with the great recommendations of a clear, bold type, and good paper, the lesser, but attractive merits, of being well illustrated and elegantly bound."—*Post.*

"This new and cheap edition of Sam Slick's popular work will be an acquisition to all lovers of wit and humour. Mr Justice Haliburton's writings are so well known that no commendation is needed. The volume is very handsomely bound and illustrated, and the paper and type are excellent. It is in every way suited for a library edition, and as the names of Messrs Hurst and Blackett warrant the character of the works to be produced in their Standard Library, we have no doubt the project will be eminently successful."—*Sun*

VOL. II.—JOHN HALIFAX, GENTLEMAN.

"This is a very good and a very interesting work. It is designed to trace the career from boyhood to age of a perfect man—a Christian gentleman, and it abounds in incident both well and highly wrought. • Throughout it is conceived in a high spirit, and written with great ability. This cheap and handsome new edition is worthy to pass freely from hand to hand as a gift book in many households."—*Examiner.*

"The new and cheaper edition of this interesting work will doubtless meet with great success. John Halifax, the hero of this most beautiful story, is no ordinary hero, and this his history is no ordinary book. It is a full-length portrait of a true gentleman, one of nature's own nobility. It is also the history of a home, and a thoroughly English one. The work abounds in incident, and many of the scenes are full of graphic power and true pathos. It is a book that few will read without becoming wiser and better.—*Scotsman.*

"'John Halifax' is more than worthy of the author's reputation. We consider, indeed, that it is her best work. There are in it many passages of beautiful writing. The closing scenes are deeply pathetic, and few will lay down the book without tearful eyes. 'John Halifax' is a picture, drawn with a masterly hand, of one of nature's gentlemen. Everybody who ever reads a novel should read this one."—*Critic.*

"The story is very interesting. The attachment between John Halifax and his wife is beautifully painted, as are the pictures of their domestic life, and the growing up of their children, and the conclusion of the book is beautiful and touching."—*Athenæum.*

"John Halifax is one of the noblest stories among modern works of fiction. The interest of the story is enthralling, the characters admirably sustained, and the moral excellent."—*Press.*

"In 'John Halifax' every character is consistently conceived and very truthfully delineated. The incidents, the scenes, the 'still life,' are painted with a power that sustains the attention of the reader."—*Spectator.*

"If the delineation of the grand in character, the glorious in action, the tender in feeling, the pure in heart, can bestow eminence on a production, this work must take its place among the standard and the excellent."—*Sun.*

[CONTINUED ON THE FOLLOWING PAGES.]

HURST AND BLACKETT'S STANDARD LIBRARY
(CONTINUED).

VOL. III.—THE CRESCENT AND THE CROSS.
BY ELIOT WARBURTON.

"Independent of its value as an original narrative, and its useful and interesting information, this work is remarkable for the colouring power and play of fancy with which its descriptions are enlivened. Among its greatest and most lasting charms is its reverent and serious spirit."—*Quarterly Review.*

"A book calculated to prove more practically useful was never penned than 'The Crescent and the Cross'—a work which surpasses all others in its homage for the sublime and its love for the beautiful in those famous regions consecrated to everlasting immortality in the annals of the prophets, and which no other writer has ever depicted with a pencil at once so reverent and so picturesque."—*Sun.*

"In the mixture of story with anecdote, information, and impression, it perhaps surpasses 'Eothen.' Innumerable passages of force, vivacity, or humour are to be found in the volumes."—*Spectator.*

VOL. IV.—NATHALIE. BY JULIA KAVANAGH.

"'Nathalie' is Miss Kavanagh's best imaginative effort. Its manner is gracious and attractive. Its matter is good. A sentiment, a tenderness, are commanded by her which are as individual as they are elegant. We should not soon come to an end were we to specify all the delicate touches and attractive pictures which place 'Nathalie' high among books of its class."—*Athenæum.*

"A tale of untiring interest, full of deep touches of human nature, exhibiting all that self-sacrificing devotion, and all that sensitive waywardness, the combination of which constitutes one of the most powerful charms, as well as one of the greatest riddles, of the female character. We have no hesitation in predicting for this delightful tale a lasting popularity, and a place in the foremost ranks of that most instructive kind of fiction—the moral novel."—*John Bull.*

"A more judicious selection than Nathalie could not have been made for Messrs Hurst and Blackett's Standard Library. The series as it advances realises our first impression, that it will be one of lasting celebrity."—*Literary Gazette.*

VOL. V.—A WOMAN'S THOUGHTS ABOUT WOMEN.
BY THE AUTHOR OF "JOHN HALIFAX, GENTLEMAN."

"A book of sound counsel. It is one of the most sensible works of its kind, well-written, true-hearted, and altogether practical. Whoever wishes to give advice to a young lady may thank the author for means of doing so."—*Examiner.*

"The author of 'John Halifax' will retain and extend her hold upon the reading and reasonable public by the merits of her present work, which bears the stamp of good sense and genial feeling."—*Guardian.*

"These thoughts are good and humane. They are thoughts we would wish women to think: they are much more to the purpose than the treatises upon the women and daughters of England, which were fashionable some years ago, and these thoughts mark the progress of opinion, and indicate a higher tone of character, and a juster estimate of woman's position."—*Athenæum.*

"This really valuable volume ought to be in every young woman's hand. It will teach her how to think and how to act. We are glad to see it in this Standard Library."—*Literary Gazette.*

"It is almost unnecessary to remark that the authoress of 'John Halifax' must almost surely write a clever book; but there are deep thoughts upon the phases of woman's conduct and disposition, in this volume, which for accuracy and excellence supersede the former productions of the same pen. The book will attract and delight those whom it does not profess to teach."—*John Bull.*

"Originating in the purest of motives,—the desire of seeing the female portion of the community virtuous, wise, useful, happy,—these thoughts are worthy of the earnest and enlightened mind, the all-embracing charity, and the well-earned reputation of the author of 'John Halifax.'"—*Herald.*

"A sensible well-written review of the true position and duties of women. There are some exceedingly valuable remarks upon female professions and handicrafts."—*Critic.*

HURST AND BLACKETT'S STANDARD LIBRARY

(CONTINUED).

VOL. VI.—ADAM GRAEME OF MOSSGRAY.
BY THE AUTHOR OF "MRS MARGARET MAITLAND."

"'Adam Graeme' is a story awakening genuine emotions of interest and delight by its admirable pictures of Scottish life and scenery. The plot is cleverly complicated, and there is great vitality in the dialogue, and remarkable brilliancy in the descriptive passages, as who that has read 'Margaret Maitland' would not be prepared to expect? But the story has a 'mightier magnet still,' in the healthy tone which pervades it, in its feminine delicacy of thought and diction, and in the truly womanly tenderness of its sentiments. The eloquent author sets before us the essential attributes of Christian virtue, their deep and silent workings in the heart, and their beautiful manifestations in the life, with a delicacy, a power, and a truth which can hardly be surpassed."—*Morning Post.*

VOL. VII.—SAM SLICK'S WISE SAWS AND MODERN INSTANCES.

"The humour of Sam Slick is inexhaustible. He is ever and everywhere a welcome visitor; smiles greet his approach, and wit and wisdom hang upon his tongue. The present production is remarkable alike for its racy humour, its sound philosophy, the felicity of its illustrations, and the delicacy of its satire. We promise our readers a great treat from the perusal of these 'Wise Saws and Modern Instances,' which contain a world of practical wisdom, and a treasury of the richest fun."—*Post.*

"We have not the slightest intention to criticise this book. Its reputation is made, and will stand as long as that of Scott's or Bulwer's Novels. The remarkable originality of its purpose, and the happy description it affords of American life and manners, still continue the subject of universal admiration. To say thus much is to say enough, though we must just mention that the new edition forms a part of the Publishers' Cheap Standard Library, which has included some of the very best specimens of light literature that ever have been written."—*Messenger.*

VOL. VIII.—CARDINAL WISEMAN'S RECOLLECTIONS OF THE LAST FOUR POPES.

"A picturesque book on Rome and its ecclesiastical sovereigns, by an eloquent Roman Catholic. Cardinal Wiseman has here treated a special subject with so much generality and geniality, that his recollections will excite no ill-feeling in those who are most conscientiously opposed to every idea of human infallibility represented in Papal domination."—*Athenæum.*

VOL. IX.—A LIFE FOR A LIFE.
BY THE AUTHOR OF "JOHN HALIFAX, GENTLEMAN."

"We are always glad to welcome Miss Muloch. She writes from her own convictions, and she has the power not only to conceive clearly what it is that she wishes to say, but to express it in language effective and vigorous. In 'A Life for a Life' she is fortunate in a good subject, and she has produced a work of strong effect. The reader having read the book through for the story, will be apt (if he be of our persuasion) to return and read again many pages and passages with greater pleasure than on a first perusal. The whole book is replete with a graceful, tender delicacy; and in addition to its other merits, it is written in good careful English."—*Athenæum.*

"The works of this author go beneath the surface, and present a picture of human joys and human sufferings in which those deep hopes, disappointments, and sorrows, which are the very well-springs of our existence, are brought to light, and set before us by a sympathising mind. 'A Life for a Life' is a book of this class. The characters are depicted with a masterly hand, the events are dramatically set forth; the descriptions of scenery and sketches of society are admirably penned; moreover the work has an object—a clearly defined moral—most poetically, most beautifully drawn; and through all there is that strong reflective mind visible which lays bare the human heart and human mind to the very core."—*Post.*

HURST AND BLACKETT'S STANDARD LIBRARY

(CONTINUED).

VOL. X.—THE OLD COURT SUBURB. BY LEIGH HUNT.

"A delightful book, of which the charm begins at the first line on the first page, for full of quaint and pleasant memories is the phrase that is its title, 'The Old Court Suburb.' Very full, too, both of quaint and pleasant memories is the line that designates the author. It is the name of the most cheerful of chroniclers, the best of remembrancers of good things, the most polished and entertaining of educated gossips. 'The Old Court Suburb' is a work that will be welcome to all readers, and most welcome to those who have a love for the best kinds of reading."—*Examiner*.

"A more agreeable and entertaining book has not been published since Boswell produced his reminiscences of Johnson."—*Observer*.

VOL. XI.—MARGARET AND HER BRIDESMAIDS.

"We may save ourselves the trouble of giving any lengthened review of this work, for we recommend all who are in search of a fascinating novel to read it for themselves. They will find it well worth their while. There are a freshness and originality about it quite charming, and there is a certain nobleness in the treatment both of sentiment and incident which is not often found."—*Athenæum*.

VOL. XII.—THE OLD JUDGE. BY SAM SLICK.

"This work is redolent of the hearty fun and strong masculine sense of our old friend 'Sam Slick.' In these sketches we have different interlocutors, and a far greater variety of character than in 'Sam Slick,' while in acuteness of observation, pungency of remark, and abounding heartiness of drollery, the present work of Judge Haliburton is quite equal to the first. Every page is alive with rapid, fresh sketches of character, droll, quaint, racy sayings, good-humoured practical jokes, and capitally-told anecdotes."—*Chronicle*.

"These popular sketches, in which the Author of 'Sam Slick' paints Nova Scotian life, form the 12th Volume of Messrs Hurst and Blackett's Standard Library of Modern Works. The publications included in this Library have all been of good quality; many give information while they entertain, and of that class the book before us is a specimen. The manner in which the Cheap Editions forming the series is produced deserves especial mention. The paper and print are unexceptionable; there is a steel engraving in each volume, and the outsides of them will satisfy the purchaser who likes to see a regiment of books in handsome uniform."—*Examiner*.

VOL. XIII.—DARIEN. BY ELIOT WARBURTON.

"This last production, from the pen of the author of 'The Crescent and the Cross,' has the same elements of a very wide popularity. It will please its thousands."—*Globe*.

"This work will be read with peculiar interest as the last contribution to the literature of his country of a man endowed with no ordinary gifts of intellect. Eliot Warburton's active and productive genius is amply exemplified in the present book. We have seldom met with any work in which the realities of history and the poetry of fiction were more happily interwoven."—*Illustrated News*.

VOL. XIV.—FAMILY ROMANCE; OR, DOMESTIC ANNALS OF THE ARISTOCRACY.

BY SIR BERNARD BURKE, ULSTER KING OF ARMS.

"It were impossible to praise too highly as a work of amusement this most interesting book, whether we should have regard to its excellent plan or its not less excellent execution. It ought to be found on every drawing-room table. Here you have nearly fifty captivating romances with the pith of all their interest preserved in undiminished poignancy, and any one may be read in half an hour. It is not the least of their merits that the romances are founded on fact—or what, at least, has been handed down for truth by long tradition—and the romance of reality far exceeds the romance of fiction. Each story is told in the clear, unaffected style with which the author's former works have made the public familiar."—*Standard*.

HURST AND BLACKETT'S STANDARD LIBRARY
(CONTINUED).

VOL. XV.—THE LAIRD OF NORLAW,
BY THE AUTHOR OF "MRS MARGARET MAITLAND."

"The author of this delightful work is favourably known to the reading public through several other books of the same class, but the present is, in our judgment, by far the best and most finished production of them all. Scottish life and character, in connection with the fortunes of the house of Norlaw, are here delineated with truly artistic skill. The plot of the tale is simple, but the incidents with which it is interwoven are highly wrought and dramatic in their effect, and altogether there is a fascination about the work which holds the attention spell-bound from the first page to the last."—*Herald.*

"A good reprint of Mrs Oliphant's well-known story 'The Laird of Norlaw' constitutes one of the latest additions to Messrs Hurst and Blackett's Standard Library, at five shillings the volume. All the world knows that the books contained in this series are, for the most part, works of sterling merit. Mrs Oliphant is in good company among whom she is quite able to hold her own."—*Spectator.*

"We have had frequent opportunities of commending Messrs Hurst and Blackett's Standard Library, of which this forms the fifteenth volume. For neatness, elegance, and distinctness the volumes in this series surpass anything with which we are familiar. The author of the present work has been successful to a degree in previous productions. Adam Graeme, for instance, contained some admirable pictures of Scottish life, character, and scenery, and The Laird of Norlaw will fully sustain the reputation justly acquired by that most interesting story. The reader is carried on from first to last with an energy of sympathy that never flags."—*Sunday Times.*

VOL. XVI.—THE ENGLISHWOMAN IN ITALY,
BY MRS G. GRETTON.

"Mrs Gretton had opportunities which rarely fall to the lot of strangers of becoming acquainted with the inner life and habits of a part of the Italian peninsula which is now the very centre of the national crisis. We can praise her performance as interesting, unexaggerated, and full of opportune instruction."—*The Times.*

"Mrs Gretton's book is timely, life-like, and for every reason to be recommended. It is impossible to close the book without liking the writer as well as the subject. The work is engaging, because real."—*Athenæum.*

"'The Englishwoman in Italy' is a book on which we may well congratulate both our own countrymen and the Italians, because it tells for itself that it is written by one whom both parties may regard with confidence as being in thought, feeling, and culture a representative Englishwoman, admirably qualified to interpret between them, and make them known. The book is fresh in manner and original in matter. It is as amusing as a novel, and has the solid value belonging to a faithful and lively delineation of real life."—*Spectator.*

"The *prestige* of current events was not needed to place this work among the very pleasantest and most interesting of its class, but with the added importance now attached to all relating to the people of Italy it assumes a higher position. The peculiar facilities afforded the author for entering Italian penetralia by the position and character of her uncle and host, a dweller at Ancona, are made admirable use of. The family festivals, the public amusements, the daily routine of life in all classes, are described with a simplicity and freshness which make these varied pictures of society, with their surroundings of glorious Italian skies, and waters, and scenery, truly delightful."—*Globe.*

"Mrs Gretton's book comes before the world at a most appropriate hour, and being one of the most delightful specimens of descriptive literature that we have for a long time fallen in with, will be read with general satisfaction and pleasure. The great beauty of Mrs Gretton's book is its simplicity. The author aims at no grand eloquence. She tells what she has seen and known in a manner that indicates refinement, and writes of persons and places with that easy clearness which manifests intelligence. We refer our readers to the book itself for as rich a treat as can be afforded from any class of literature in the present day."—*Messenger.*

"A graphic, thoughtful, and amusing work."—*Critic.*

HURST AND BLACKETT, PUBLISHERS, 13, GREAT MARLBOROUGH STREET.

HURST AND BLACKETT'S STANDARD LIBRARY

(CONTINUED).

VOL. XVII.—NOTHING NEW.
BY THE AUTHOR OF "JOHN HALIFAX, GENTLEMAN."
Illustrated by J. E. MILLAIS, A.R.A.

"We cordially commend this book. The same graphic power, deep pathos, healthful sentiment, and masterly execution, which place that beautiful work, 'John Halifax,' among the English Classics are everywhere displayed."—*Chronicle*.

"The reader will find these narratives fully calculated to remind him of that truth and energy of human portraiture, that spell over human affections and emotions, which have stamped this author one of the first novelists of the day."—*John Bull*.

"'Nothing New' displays all those superior merits which have made 'John Halifax' one of the most popular works of the day. There is a force and truthfulness about these tales which mark them as the production of no ordinary mind, and we cordially recommend them to the perusal of all lovers of fiction."—*Post*.

"These tales, by the author of 'John Halifax,' possess that peculiar grace, terseness, and fluency, which characterize her longer stories. They cannot fail to charm."—*Globe*.

Also lately published, in 1 vol.,
STUDIES FROM LIFE.
BY THE AUTHOR OF "JOHN HALIFAX, GENTLEMAN."

"These studies are truthful and vivid pictures of life, often earnest, always full of right feeling, and occasionally lightened by touches of quiet genial humour. The volume is remarkable for thought, sound sense, shrewd observation, and kind and sympathetic feeling for all things good and beautiful."—*Post*.

"A most charming volume. One which all women and most men would be proud to possess."—*Chronicle*.

"Without being in the same degree elaborate either in purpose or plot as 'John Halifax,' these 'Studies from Life' may be pronounced to be equally as clever in construction and narration. It is one of the most charming features of Miss Mulock's works that they invariably lead to a practical and useful end. Her object is to improve the taste, refine the intellect, and touch the heart, and so to act upon all classes of her readers as to make them rise from the consideration of her books both wiser and better than they were before they began to read them. The 'Studies from Life' will add considerably to the author's well-earned reputation."—*Messenger*.

"These 'Studies from Life' are characterized by that earnest thought and warm vigour of expression which belongs to all the writer's works."—*John Bull*.

"The whole work is characterized by a high moral tone, which, in combination with the variety of the subjects, and the skill of their treatment, cannot fail to recommend the book to a wide circulation."—*Observer*.

Also lately published, in 1 vol., with Illustrations by BIRKET FOSTER,
POEMS. BY THE AUTHOR OF JOHN HALIFAX.

"We are well pleased with these Poems by our popular novelist. They are the expression of genuine thoughts, feelings, and aspirations, and the expression is almost always graceful, musical, and well-coloured. A high, pure tone of morality pervades each set of verses."—*Spectator*.

"A volume of Poems which will assuredly take its place with those of Goldsmith, Gray, and Cowper on the favourite shelf of every Englishman's library. We discover in these Poems all the firmness, vigour, and delicacy of touch which characterize the author's prose works, and, in addition, an ineffable tenderness and grace such as we find in few poetical compositions besides those of Tennyson."—*News of the World*.

"These Poems will be eagerly read by thousands. There are proofs of imaginative power in them, which forcibly remind us of Wordsworth in his best moods."—*Press*.

HURST AND BLACKETT, PUBLISHERS, 13, GREAT MARLBOROUGH STREET.

www.ingramcontent.com/pod-product-compliance
Lightning Source LLC
Chambersburg PA
CBHW032132230426
43672CB00011B/2313